DECORATING YOUR
CHILD'S ROOM

DECORATING YOUR CHILD'S ROOM

ELIZABETH KEEVILL

WARD LOCK

*To my parents, Peter and Betty Cole, with much love
and to Charlie, Luke and Sebbie, the children of my dearest friends*

A WARD LOCK BOOK

First paperback edition 1995

First published in the UK 1991 by Ward Lock
Wellington House, 125 Strand, London WC2R 0BB, England

A Cassell imprint

Copyright © Text Elizabeth Keevill 1991, 1995

Distributed in the United States
by Sterling Publishing Co., Inc.
387 Park Avenue South, New York, NY 10016–8810

Distributed in Australia
by Capricorn Link (Australia) Pty Ltd
2/13 Carrington Road, Castle Hill NSW 2154

A British Library Cataloguing in Publication Data block for this book may be obtained from the British Library

ISBN 0 7063 7450 9

Typeset in England by RGM, The Mews, Birkdale Village, Southport
Printed and bound in Spain by Graficromo S.A. Cordoba

Author's Note: The male personal pronoun has been used throughout this book in accordance with the publisher's style. The text applies equally to both sexes in all cases.

> **Approximate imperial measurement conversions have been given as a guide, but follow the metric measurements throughout if possible.**

A small all-over nursery print on a light background has been chosen to decorate the upper parts of the walls and the ceiling of this nursery. It successfully unifies the odd-shaped walls and contrasts effectively with the plain painted wood panelling which reaches up to dado height. A co-ordinating wallpaper border, just below the dado rail, links the two halves of the wall. Using a pale colour scheme is important in a room like this, where there is a limited amount of natural light.

CONTENTS

INTRODUCTION

Decorating and furnishing a room for a new baby or small child is probably the most enjoyable and potentially creative of all home furnishing projects. And a carefully thought-out, special room scheme also reflects the fact that every child, from the moment it is born, is unique.

Because nurseries and their furnishings are often small they are the best areas of the home for experimenting with new ideas and techniques such as paint effects, patchwork and stencilling. And if you do not get absolutely perfect results, the new occupant will not be too fussy! You can also be more experimental with your combinations of

colours and patterns than in any other room in the house and, although certain suggestions are made in the book about colour scheming and putting together a room scheme, feel free to break all the rules — they are only suggestions after all!

The emphasis is on a bold and colourful, rather than soft and frilly, approach to decorating a nursery, and this is not just personal taste but is based on scientific research into which colours a child perceives first, and what he finds visually stimulating. Lots of frills and flounces can make life complicated, and not just when you are making up the items. Everything in a nursery

will end up getting dirty at some time or another and you do not want to make extra work for yourself by having to wash and iron fiddly trimmings.

Before the birth is the best time to work on

If you choose fabric and wallpaper from a range of co-ordinating patterns, consider taking a mix-and-match approach and combine a variety of prints and colours together in the same room. Provided they have colours and some pattern elements in common, such a mix can be highly effective and creates plenty of interest and excitement. But despite the profusion of pattern, the overall effect here is subtle and certainly does not dominate the room or overpower the child's possessions.

The colour theme is predominantly blue, with touches of green, red and yellow, all on a cream background. Wallpaper, plus a border, and fabrics with strong patterns and motifs are balanced by plainer striped paper and gingham check fabric. The curtains are lined with yellow check fabric, and bound at the edges with blue tape. Oxford pillowcases are made from the check fabric and a comforter has been lined and bound with the same design. Cushions allow the bed to be used as a sitting area during the day.

The bedstead and bookcase have been hand-dragged (a decorative paint effect) in blue, which is an excellent way to bring older pieces of furniture up-to-date. Remember that children should not be given second-hand mattresses and bed-bases to sleep on and that it is important to budget for the best quality beds that you can afford. This bed has been fitted with a new divan base which slips into the well of the bed and rests on the side and end rails. These 'well bed-bases' are made-to-measure to order and enable you to combine antique furniture with up-to-the-minute comfort.

the room's decor and accessories. Once the baby is born there probably won't be many spare moments, so this book is aimed mainly at expectant first-time mothers and their partners. As this may be the first time couples have embarked on home decorating, I have assumed little prior knowledge on the subject. Also, because new parents often have to work to a limited budget, the emphasis is on investing time, energy and ideas, rather than money.

But there is also much that parents of toddlers and children up to four will find inspirational. Parents expecting second and subsequent children may be even more budget conscious than the first time around, so they will find the ideas for adapting and revamping particularly useful. Older children may have great fun in lending a hand, as well as being involved with the new child in a positive way.

Of course, how things look is very important, but it is absolutely essential where young children are involved that things are practical, and above all safe. Although many countries have regulations covering the design and manufacture of merchandise for babies and children, when you are making things yourself you do not have government legislation to fall back on, so follow instructions in the text very carefully. Within the necessary practical and safety considerations it is still possible to create a lively, stimulating and attractive scheme. Additional safety information will be found in the room-by-room safety appendix at the end of the book.

You will find information on what items are absolutely essential for a nursery and what are optional extras which may enhance your enjoyment of your new baby, but which the baby will not miss should you choose to omit them.

As a safety note, pregnant women should be very careful when decorating, particularly when climbing ladders or using certain materials such as spray paint or paint stripper. If you are in any doubt about the suitability of a certain activity, always seek advice from the manufacturer of the product or from your midwife or doctor.

Co-ordinating ranges of wallpapers, borders and fabrics make easy work of choosing the decoration for a child's room. This one has a cute character on the fabric and border, which co-ordinate with a plainer wallpaper. The border has been applied immediately above the dado rail, which is at a good height for a child to enjoy. Although the woodwork has been painted white, it could just as effectively have been painted in the yellow, or either of the two blues found in the design. Mix-to-order paint ranges are the best way to match colours for this purpose.

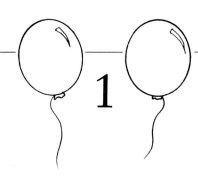

1

COLOUR SCHEMING

Nowadays babies often sleep in their parents' bedrooms for the first few weeks or months. This simplifies night-time feeds, makes keeping a check on your baby easier and is more reassuring for him. However, some people find it difficult to sleep with a baby in the same room so, if you have the space, you may prefer to put him in his own room at night from the start.

Even if you decide to have your baby in with you for the first few months, it is a good idea to prepare a separate nursery for him in advance of the birth. Once the baby is born you will have lots of baby things, such as clothes, nappies, toys and bedding, which need a home and which might be better stored in a room other than your bedroom. You may also prefer to put him in his own room for daytime sleeps and you may prefer to bathe and change him in there too. Once he is three or four months old, though, he will begin to take more notice of your movements and you are likely to wake him as you walk around your bedroom, so at this point you should think about moving him into his own room.

If you do not have room in your home for a separate nursery you will need somewhere in your bedroom to put other baby items plus, ideally, somewhere to change nappies. It makes life easier if you can actually put aside part of your room and have everything together in one place. Being organized, in this way, saves you having to dash around the room getting things together just to change a nappy, for example. It is best to put the cot on the side of the room away from the door so that you do not have to walk past it whenever you go in or out. A free-standing, waist-height storage unit can also be used as a room divider if you have space. As well as visually dividing the room into two parts it also provides storage space and a nappy changing surface at the same time. If you are really short of space, you can, of course, use the bedroom solely for sleeping and carry out the other activities elsewhere in the house.

When you are deciding which bedroom should become the nursery, do not automatically opt for the smallest bedroom, just because a baby is small! Children spend more time in their rooms than adults; they will play and store their possessions in there, unless they are lucky enough to have a separate play room. Later on they will want to use the room as a study and for entertaining friends.

As regards the position of the room, if it is possible to have a choice, the most suitable situation for a baby's room is close to yours and also to the bathroom. If you intend to have a loft conversion to gain extra space, avoid making it the baby's room — you will not want to climb extra steps carrying a baby, and also it is an extra flight of stairs for your child to negotiate once he starts walking.

It is advisable to work out the colour scheme for the nursery well before the child is born so that you can get most of the decorating out of the way and, in particular, allow any paint fumes time to disperse. This means that, unless you know the sex of your child already (if you have had amniocentesis, for example), you will need to opt for a basically neuter colour scheme, rather than pink or pale blue. Once the child is born you can then add pink or pale blue in easy-to-do ways if you want, such as with wallpaper borders, cushion covers and accessories. For a while after the baby is born you will be hard pushed to find the time or energy for any more decorating anyway.

But besides being rather stereotyped, pink and pale blue are not terribly stimulating colours for a newborn baby. Although he can see and is particularly sensitive to movement, he will not be able to focus on anything further than about 25–30 cm (10–12 in) away at first, neither will he be able to detect colour. Once he begins to detect colour, he will only see very bright colours so it is a good idea to include these colours into a baby's room scheme if it is to provide visual stimulation. Red and blue are the first colours he will see, then green and yellow. But as a bedroom is also supposed to be relaxing, aim for colours and designs that are cheerful rather than garish. Eyesight will develop properly when the child is three to six months old.

The basic principles of a colour scheme for a child's room are the same as those for any other room. These principles can be very useful to get inspiration and help you to decide on the most appropriate, and perhaps original, way to decorate. You may think this is taking the decoration of a child's room rather too seriously, but it can be a fun way to come up with ideas and makes a good starting point.

It is also important to be practical about a room scheme for a baby. Unless you have a big budget and will have time to change the scheme again soon, avoid obviously babyish schemes with lots of lavish frills and lace which would only be suitable for a year or so. Flounces and fancy trims are not only time consuming to sew, but also to wash and iron, since they will inevitably get dirty. These sorts of schemes are really much more for the benefit of the parents than for the child, but if your heart is set on it, and you do not mind redecorating fairly soon, do not be deterred!

It makes more sense to plan with future changes in mind, and aim for a basic room scheme which will be flexible enough to last for several years. Avoid trapping yourself into a rigid scheme and make any baby elements of an easy-to-change nature. Wallpaper borders, for example, can be easily stripped off and replaced with something more grown up, stencilling can be painted over, bed linen, rugs and cushion covers can easily be changed as can pictures. Changing paint, wallcoverings, curtains, blinds and flooring may be less acceptable, so decide how often you are prepared to redecorate and which things you are prepared to replace in the near future as this will affect your choice of room scheme.

COLOUR THEORY

An understanding of simple colour theory can be a great help when choosing colours, and the colour wheel is the best way to understand the way colour works and how colour schemes are put together generally. The primary colours — red, yellow and blue — are the most important on the wheel because, in theory, all other colours can be mixed from them. Between the primaries are found the secondary colours: green, orange and purple. These colours are made by mixing two primaries together. Each secondary colour is positioned between the two primary colours from which it is mixed, for example, purple is mixed from red and blue and so is therefore found between these two colours on the wheel.

Tertiary colours are a mixture of a primary and a secondary colour. An example is turquoise, which is made from blue and green. Colour also comes in different tones, which means that black or white has been added to the original colour in varying degrees. Colour to which white has been added is called a pastel or a tint — pink, for example, is a tint of red. And colour which has had black added to it is a shade — navy, for example, is a dark version of blue. Shades of grey do not appear on the wheel, because black and white are not strictly colours, but greys are very important in colour schemes all the same.

Colour is further divided into 'warm' and 'cold'. Oranges, reds, yellows and their variations make up the warm colours, so-called because they are associated with sunshine and firelight. Blues, greens and their derivatives are cold colours, because they are linked with ice and water.

The main types of colour scheme are based on their relation to each other on the colour wheel. They are suggestions to be used as a basis for ideas, and there is nothing to stop you adding accent colours (bright, contrasting colours) in small amounts to bring more life and interest to your schemes.

Monochromatic schemes are based on one or more shades of the same colour, such as a mixture of neutrals, tones of pink and maroon or tones of ultramarine, navy and pale blue. This is the easiest type of colour scheme and is quite a good choice for a child's room because it is easy to add interest with wallpaper borders and stencilling, or with accessories such as posters, pictures, cushions and bedlinen in accent colours. The presence of these strong colours is particularly important for babies. A monochromatic scheme also provides a background for the older child's pictures and possessions without dominating them. A mixture of pastel colours also makes a good colour scheme, because from whichever part of the colour wheel the colours are taken, they will still co-ordinate.

Related or harmonious schemes are based on two or three toning colours found next to each other on the colour wheel. These colours work well together because they are closely related and so will not clash or dominate. Small amounts of an accent colour, such as red, can bring extra interest.

Opposite or contrasting schemes are based on colours found directly opposite each other on the colour wheel, such as orange and blue or red and green. These pairs of colours are called 'complementaries' and, when placed together, they intensify each other. In other words, green surrounded by red looks even greener. Colours used in their purest forms in this type of colour scheme can be rather overwhelming so they tend to be used in fairly small quantities, as accents, with the rest of the colour in the form of tints.

A variation on the contrasting scheme is to team a colour with those lying immediately to either side of its complementary, such as orange with blue-green or blue-violet. This arrangement is known as a 'split complementary'.

Triads, which are any three colours equidistant apart on the wheel, also harmonize. The best example of this is the primary colours — red, blue and yellow. These are a particularly good choice for babies because they are the colours they can see first, and therefore they are more stimulating than the traditional pastels.

Whichever colour scheme you choose, and even if you choose not to follow a particular type of colour scheme, it is important to bear in mind that colour looks most balanced in a room scheme when it is used in unequal proportions, however contradictory that may sound. Equal quantities of different colours in a room scheme will look clumsy, and if the colours are fairly strong the effect can be very oppressive. Pick one colour to dominate, another to feature in rather smaller amounts, and one or two more to appear as accents.

To gain inspiration for your colour scheme, look through home-interest books, catalogues and magazines. Collect the colour cards that paint manufacturers supply. These often have useful information on colour scheming and show the main colours for that year grouped in very attractive ways. Even a postcard or a picture can be an inspiration if you like the overall colour effect and think that it is suitable for your child's room.

A multi-coloured fabric or wallpaper is often the starting point for a colour scheme. It could just as easily be a cushion cover or bed quilt. Pick out the individual colours in the form of paint and other furnishings, and use the colours in similar proportions to those on the original fabric or wallpaper. Experiment with mixing patterns — very simple patterns such as stripes, spots and gingham checks can make successful companion fabrics to strong patterns. In fact, having a mixture of co-ordinating patterns in a room scheme is often the secret of its success as it gives a busy and casual effect — just the right emphasis for a child's room.

Some manufacturers make it very easy to

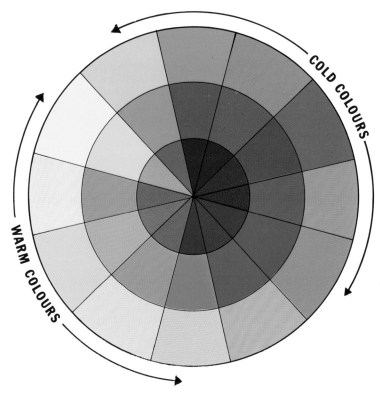

achieve a co-ordinated look by supplying a wide range of co-ordinating merchandise and doing all the hard work for you. These ranges usually include wallpaper, borders, fabric, bedlinen and other decorations.

But you do not have to opt for one of these collections in order to have a co-ordinated look. In fact, if you do it all by yourself, you will end up with something far more interesting and original.

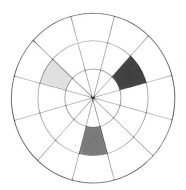
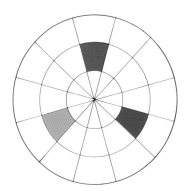
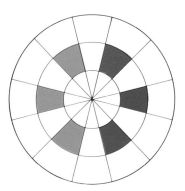

Colour Theory

Unless you know the sex of your child before it is born and decide to go for pink or pale blue, it is safest to settle on a neutral colour scheme so that you can get on with the decorating well before the birth. This is important because you want to minimize the chances of exposing your newborn baby to paint fumes.

For this room, a monochromatic scheme based around tones of yellow has been chosen. Being neutral, yellow is particularly popular for babies' rooms. It is cheerful, sunny and fresh and is easy to liven up with other primary colours. Yet in addition to all these qualities, yellow also gives a soft and gentle touch. Eggshell paint was chosen for the woodwork to enhance the soft effect and a paler, primrose yellow vinyl silk emulsion (an easier type of paint to keep clean than vinyl matt) was chosen for the walls. Tiny touches of the other two primaries, red and blue, have been introduced in the stencilled border, in the rug and in the cushion cover. While only being present in small amounts, they inject extra life and interest into the scheme and prevent it from appearing monotonous.

What this picture demonstrates perfectly is that it is possible to create a delightful and very personal room for your child without buying any special baby furniture apart from a cot, and without covering every available surface with baby motifs which the child will grow out of quickly. The couple who decorated this room did so on a limited budget and wanted to leave it as long as possible before they decorated again so they chose a room scheme that was adaptable. The main source of pattern comes from the jolly stencilled duck frieze just below the ceiling. Fun and cheap to do, it can easily be painted over when outgrown or covered with a wide wallpaper border.

Furniture was cleverly adapted and recycled. The low chest of drawers on the left, under the window, had been in the family for years. It makes a good surface, at a comfortable height, for changing a baby and a padded changing mat has been chosen to fit the top exactly.

A chest of drawers combined with a small cupboard, bought from a second-hand shop, has been painted with eggshell paint and given a new lease of life with some smart porcelain handles. This is an ideal piece of furniture for a small child's room as babies' clothes tend to fold up in

drawers, rather than be hung up. The top half, fitted with a rail, is sufficiently tall to take hanging clothes for several years.

Cheerful yellow and white fabrics in co-ordinating stripes and checks have been chosen for the curtains and chair covers. These fabrics tie in with the room scheme beautifully yet are suitable for several years of use as they are not specifically baby-oriented. The simple lined curtains, topped with a traditional pelmet, have been teamed with a special opaque plain yellow blind (just hidden from view) in order to keep out as much light as possible. The piped slip-on seat covers with gathered skirts bring new life to two second-hand occasional chairs and are simple to remove for washing.

The couple decided on carpet for the floor. Being a small room, the outlay was not large and they felt that warmth and comfort underfoot was important. But bearing in mind that there would probably be spills and accidents, they chose a nylon carpet which has special stain-resistant properties. Such carpets, however, are not stain-proof and spills need to be dealt with straight away if staining is not to occur.

PUTTING TOGETHER A SAMPLE BOARD

When interior designers are planning a room scheme they put together a 'sample board'. This consists of a room plan, pictures from magazines and catalogues plus colour samples of wallpaper, paint, fabric and flooring, all mounted on a sheet of card for presentation to the client. This is an excellent way for anyone, not just an interior designer, to approach interior decoration.

1 Draw a sketch map of the room, marking in the measurements in metric and imperial (some merchandise is still sold in imperial measurements), the height of the room and the size and position of windows. This will be very handy for calculating the amount of wallpaper, paint, carpet and curtain fabric you will need. Also mark in the position of lights, plug sockets and switches, any furniture or furnishings that are to remain in the room, and also the north-south axis. The reason for this is that rooms facing north, for example, need different treatment from those facing south.

2 Collect together cuttings from magazines and brochures showing the sort of effect you want to achieve, plus your fabric cuttings, paint charts, wallpaper and flooring samples.

3 Pick out the samples that work best together and provide the effect you are looking for and mount them on the board. If possible try to get samples which are roughly in proportion to the room's furnishings. For example, the floor or wall-covering sample will probably be the largest.

4 Glue the cuttings, sketch map and samples together on a piece of stiff white card measuring about 25 × 35 cm (10 × 14 in). Butt the samples up together so there are no white gaps between them. You will now have an instant reference guide to the room scheme which you can take with you when you are shopping for other items.

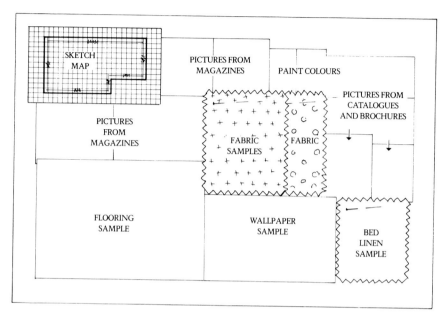

Once you have more or less decided on the scheme see if you can borrow large swatches of the fabrics, wallpapers and flooring and put them in the actual room for a few days. That way you can see whether you can live with them, as initially you will be spending a lot of time in your child's room so it is important that you like the design. Later when you come to redecorate, your child will probably want to have a hand in choosing the room scheme and will express preferences for certain furnishings and designs. Make sure that, on a large scale, they still look good together, and also check their appearance under the natural and artificial light in the room as colours can vary dramatically under different conditions and at different times of the day.

If you are unable to borrow swatches, consider buying a length of fabric or a roll of wallpaper before you commit yourself to buying enough for the whole room. You may save yourself a considerable amount of money if it does not look right *in situ*. Some stores will exchange unopened rolls of wallpaper.

The large paint companies have made

Putting together a sample board is an excellent way to organise your thoughts when planning the decor for a nursery or child's room. It is also good discipline, especially if you are on a tight budget, because you are much less likely to make impulse buys which you may later regret. Older children will enjoy helping to put a board together for their room and this is a good way for them to learn about colour co-ordination.

paint easy to sample. They sell trial pots of their most popular colours which contain enough paint to cover about 2 square metres (yards). You can try it out on the wall, live with it for a few days, and if you decide you do not like it then paint it over. Alternatively paint a large sheet of thick white card with your chosen paint. That way you can move it around the room and see how it looks in the shady parts of the room, as well as in the direct light from the window. If you have chosen paint which is not available in a tester pot, consider buying the smallest quantity that is produced. Again, if it turns out to be unsuitable you have not wasted as much money as if you had bought enough for the entire room.

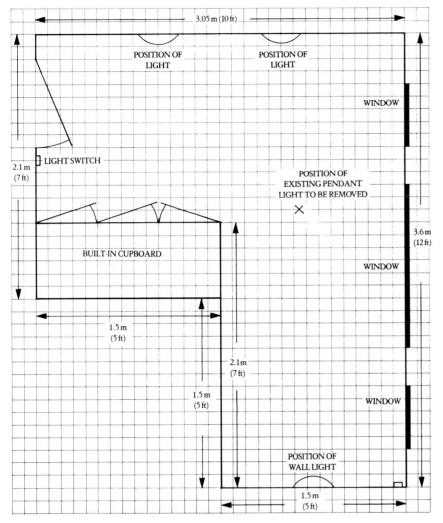

3.05 m (10 ft)

POSITION OF LIGHT

POSITION OF LIGHT

WINDOW

LIGHT SWITCH

2.1 m (7 ft)

POSITION OF EXISTING PENDANT LIGHT TO BE REMOVED

×

3.6 m (12 ft)

BUILT-IN CUPBOARD

WINDOW

1.5 m (5 ft)

2.1 m (7 ft)

1.5 m (5 ft)

WINDOW

POSITION OF WALL LIGHT

1.5 m (5 ft)

A floor plan, marked with measurements in both imperial and metric measurements is an invaluable aid when you are budgeting for materials for your baby's room. It is also useful for planning the position of lighting and furniture. Include a copy of it on your sample board and take the whole lot with you when you go shopping.

PROBLEM ROOMS

In the same way that not all clothes suit a given person, not all colour schemes are suitable for a particular room. No room is perfect, so choosing the most appropriate scheme for a room is important to flatter its good points, disguise or draw attention away from weak points and help the room look its best.

○ North- or east-facing rooms should be decorated in warm colours such as yellow or pink.

○ South- or west-facing rooms can be decorated with cool colours such as blues and greens.

○ Rooms whose windows are overshadowed by trees or other buildings or because the room is in a basement, benefit from being decorated with pale, warm colours.

○ Small rooms can either be decorated in pale and/or cool colours to make them larger — cool colours recede and appear to push the walls further away from you.

○ Choosing a furnishing fabric in a colour and/or pattern to match the walls helps make the room look more spacious.

○ A low ceiling can be made to look higher by painting it a lighter colour than the walls.

○ Vertical stripes make a room appear taller.

○ A light-coloured floor will make a room appear larger.

○ Larger rooms can be made to appear smaller and cosier by decorating them in warm and/or strong or dark colours — warm colours give the illusion of bringing surfaces nearer to you. Bold wallpaper patterns have the same effect.

○ A high ceiling can be made to look lower by painting it in a rich, dark colour, bringing the colour down to the picture rail, if there is one. Do not choose a very dark colour though or it will look oppressive. Matching the ceiling colour to the flooring helps balance the effect.

○ Horizontal stripes make a room appear wider.

○ To make a long, thin room look a more normal shape, paint the narrow walls in a warm and/or dark colour to make it appear nearer.

○ If a room has lots of odd angles, decorate the walls and ceiling in the same colour to make it look less bitty. Using a wallpaper with a tiny, unfussy print helps camouflage the odd-shaped walls and ceiling even more.

○ Paint pipes or radiators the same colour as the wall behind to disguise them.

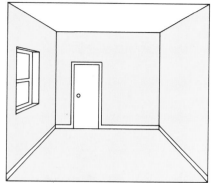

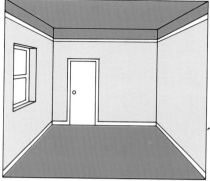

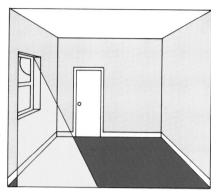

Small rooms look larger when decorated with pale and/or cool colours (avoid cool colours in a north-facing room). Painting the ceiling a lighter colour than the walls makes the room appear taller. A light-coloured floor will also make the room look larger.

Decorating a room with warm colours will make it look smaller and cosier, while painting the ceiling a rich dark colour helps it look lower. Choosing a flooring in the same colour helps balance the effect.

Sunny, south-facing rooms can take a cool colour scheme.

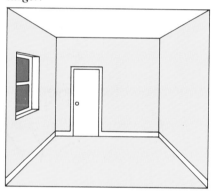

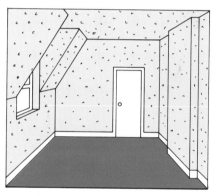

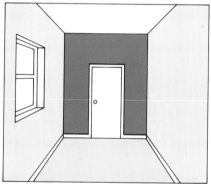

North-facing or overshadowed rooms benefit from warm sunny colours in fairly light, bright tones.

Odd-shaped rooms are given a sense of unity by decorating them with the same colour on walls and ceiling. A mini-print wallpaper helps the effect even more.

Long thin rooms can be made to look a more normal shape by painting the narrow walls with a warm and/or dark colour. A light floor covering helps give a spacious look.

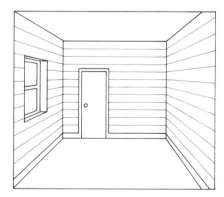

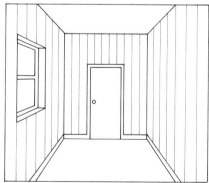

Horizontal lines make a room appear wider.

Vertical stripes make a low-ceilinged room look taller.

Children's rooms and nurseries tend to be sited in funny little odd-shaped rooms. Short of getting in the builders and moving walls, you may think that there is no way of making such rooms look acceptable. However there is much that can be done with colour and pattern to improve their appearance. Remember that you can combine visual tricks if you have more than one problem in a room. Also bear in mind that the scale of any pattern should match the size of the room — use tiny designs in small rooms and bigger ones in larger areas.

Although some children love being surrounded by lots of bright, busy patterns, others do not. Too dominating a scheme also leaves little room for the older child to make his own stamp on the room, especially if the child likes to have his masterpieces proudly displayed on the wall. So it is important to take your child's personality and preferences into account when choosing his room scheme.

This room is an excellent example of how effective a monochromatic colour scheme can be. Such a scheme combines tonal variations of the same colour — in other words light, medium and dark, in different proportions. The subtle, soft pink used here is enhanced and emphasized by the candy-striped bed linen and dusty pink carpet. A change of colour emphasis in the room can be achieved simply by changing the design of bed-linen, adding accessories and pictures in another colour and perhaps a rug on the floor.

Another benefit of a low-key colour scheme, as with this little room, is that it gives it a spacious look. Fitted furniture makes the best use of space in small rooms and here an alcove has been put to good use and has created an attractive feature. Painting furniture the same colour has also helped the feeling of space.

An excellent starting point for a colour scheme is an inspiring fabric. This stunning design, with its companion border fabric, offers plenty of scope for a child's room as there is lots going on in the design and a wide choice of colours that can be picked out for other parts of the scheme such as flooring, paintwork, bed linen, wallpaper and accessories. The fabric itself can be used to make curtains and blinds, cushion covers, comforters, tidy bags, and borders for sheets, pillowcases and towels. It also gives great inspiration for painted and stencilled designs, both on furniture and walls, motifs for mobiles and also provides stunning appliqué motifs for use on co-ordinating plain or striped fabrics. Before using fabrics to cover upholstery, check that they comply with fire regulations.

2

WALLS

To choose paint or wallcoverings for your child's room? Each style has its advantages and disadvantages which will be discussed in this chapter. All the practical aspects are considered to make an attractive and safe environment for your child. Firstly, we will look at painting in some detail.

PAINTING

Paint is the cheapest, simplest and most practical finish for the walls and ceiling of a child's room (as well as for the woodwork, of course). Modern paints are of a very high standard and can take pretty tough treatment, provided that you choose a good make and do the job properly. Paint can be washed, even scrubbed, to get rid of dirty marks. And even if paintwork does get damaged, it is a simple job to touch in the area. Most interior paints are also non-toxic, which is very important where children are involved, but double-check this is the case before you buy.

Paint is also quick to apply (especially if you use one of the new one-coat paints, see below) and it protects surfaces, making them easy to clean. It also brings colour to the room and there are a huge number of colours to choose from. If you cannot find quite the colour you want from their standard colour ranges, several major paint companies have mix-while-you-wait ranges which have hundreds of tones to choose from. These ranges are particularly useful if you are trying to match a paint with a fabric or wall-paper. Paint also has strong creative potential as it can be used for painting murals and for paint effects such as stencilling and sponging.

Just as important as finding the right colour and effect for your child's room is finding the type of paint that will best stand up to the demands that will be made on it. There may seem to be a confusing number of paints available but they basically fall into two main types — solvent-based and water-based. Both are made from the same basic ingredients: pigment, which gives the paint its colour and covering-power; binder (which is usually resin) which sticks the pigment together and to the surface to be painted; and a thinner, which is either a solvent or water.

Solvent-based paints

These are used on wood and metal. They are also known as 'oil-based', but paint formulations have changed and this expression is no longer strictly accurate. Solvent-based paints are those which require you to clean your brushes after use with white spirit or special brush cleaner. These paints are usually based on a three-part system and for best results you should buy from the same system, although you probably will not need all three parts.

The first part, primer, is only necessary if you are painting over untreated metal or wood. It soaks into the surface and gives a smooth, uniform base. Bare metal should be clean and grease-free before painting. Bare wood should be filled if necessary (see below), rubbed down and any knots painted over with patent 'knotting' before priming to prevent resin bleeding through and spoiling the top coat.

Undercoat goes on next. It is opaque and quite thick, to cover the colour underneath well and give a good, smooth surface which will be easy to sand. Undercoat is not needed if you are painting over sound, old paint of a similar colour, but you will need it if you are changing colour significantly, or if you are using liquid gloss. However, undercoat is not suitable for use on radiators or hot pipes so opt for non-drip gloss or eggshell, or special brush-on or spray-on radiator enamel.

The top coat goes on last, protecting the underneath layers and giving a decorative, easy-to-clean finish. You can choose between a gloss finish or a more matt eggshell finish. Eggshell has a lovely soft effect, but it is not quite so easy to keep clean and not quite so durable as gloss paint so it is less suitable (although not unsuitable) for a child's room. However, eggshell is the recommended finish if you intend to carry out paint effects and it can also be used on walls to give a particularly tough and durable finish (see below). Gloss comes in a non-drip form also known as gel paint, which is easiest for beginners as it will not splash or run, and also in liquid gloss form, which gives a better finish but which requires more skill to make it look good.

Water-based paints

Emulsion paint is the usual choice for walls and ceilings. It is water-based, so you can clean your brushes out under the tap. As with solvent-based paint, the more shiny the finish the easier it is to keep clean, so choose vinyl silk emulsion rather than vinyl matt for children's rooms. However, the more shiny a surface, the more it is likely to show up imperfections, so if you have rather bumpy walls you may prefer to choose vinyl matt. Modern emulsions are very durable, but if you think you need something even tougher, paint the walls with eggshell. If you like you can paint just half-way up the wall (the 'sticky finger zone'), dividing the wall with a chair rail, wallpaper border or stencilled design, and decorate above with emulsion or wallpaper.

A fairly recent innovation is roller paint. This is emulsion (both vinyl matt and vinyl silk) in a solid, jelly-like form, ready packaged in a paint tray. It is non-drip so is very easy to apply, and all you need is a roller. However, it is only available in white and a limited range of colours. Some manufacturers have now introduced high-opacity, one-coat paints, which do away with the need for undercoats and second coats, thus saving time. These are available in vinyl matt and vinyl silk emulsions and drip-resistant gloss, and have the added advantage that they are low-odour which is an important consideration as far as children and pregnant women are concerned.

PREPARING CEILINGS, WALLS AND WOODWORK

Walls must be properly prepared before they can be papered or painted — and that includes murals and paint effects. Walls should be smooth, clean and dry. Preparation work is time well spent — skimp here and the end result will look shoddy.

There is unlikely to be a lot of furniture in a future nursery but if there is, move out as much as possible before you decorate. If you cannot move it out, then group it in the middle of the room and cover it with dust sheets or old curtains. Take down blinds, curtains, curtain tracks and lampshades. Take up floor coverings if this is practicable, or cover it with polythene and then dust sheets. Dust sheets provide a useful, absorbent top layer but the polythene is important as paint may soak through on to the underlying flooring. Set aside some work clothes for yourself but avoid jumpers — they create fluff, which may stick to wet paint. Cover your hair with an old headscarf when painting the ceiling, and wear goggles. Wear a pair of old shoes while you are working. Take them off as you go out of the room and leave them by the door, so you do not tread paint through the house.

New plaster Must be clean and dry. Wipe off any salts (known as efflorescence) with a *dry* cloth; do not attempt to wash them off or the salts will be absorbed back into the wall. Wait until salts cease to form on the surface, then decorate with emulsion, priming first with a watered-down coat. Plaster should be at least a year old before being wallpapered or painted with oil-based paint. If you eventually decide to wallpaper you must treat the surface with proprietary 'size' or wallpaper paste, suitable for the type of paper you have chosen (e.g. a fungicidal paste if you are going to hang vinyl).

New wood Rub down, paint over knots with 'knotting' to prevent resin bleeding through, then give a coat of primer.

Bare metal Remove grease and oil with white spirit, prime with metal primer. Do not use undercoat on radiators or hot pipes.

Previously papered walls and ceilings Should have all traces of wallpaper removed, although lining paper and relief wall-coverings can be painted over several times as long as it is sound and still firmly fixed. Strippable paper such as vinyl is peeled off, starting at a bottom corner. The backing paper can be left behind, provided it is in good condition and is well stuck to the wall, and can be papered or painted over. Otherwise paper should be removed by damping it with a mild solution of household detergent and water. Apply it with a sponge, working from the top of the wall down. Turn the electricity off at the mains before working round plug sockets and light switches. Use a broad-bladed scraper to remove the paper, being careful not to dig into the plaster with it. If the paper is stuck to plasterboard be very careful not to overwet it or the board may swell. Paper that has been painted over or which has a waterproof surface may need scraping with a wire brush to allow the water or steam to penetrate, but be careful not to scratch into the plaster underneath. For really tough paper you may need a steam stripping machine (which can be borrowed from tool hire shops) or liquid wallpaper stripper. Finally, wash down the walls with hot water to remove any last little bits.

Previously painted walls and woodwork If they are in good condition wash them down with warm water plus a dash of washing-up liquid, to remove grease and dirt. Change the water as it gets dirty. Alternatively use sugar soap, following the directions on the container. Always work from the floor upwards so that water will not run down and cause streaks. Ceilings can be cleaned with a sponge mop. Rinse with clean, plain water and allow time to dry. If a creamy residue comes off on your sponge or cloth as you wash down the walls or ceiling, it means they have been previously painted with distemper or whitewash. It is not possible to paint over these finishes so you will have to remove it by scrubbing with a stiff brush and plain water, changing the water frequently. Finish by washing over with a detergent solution.

If the walls are in poor condition, remove any flaking or loose paint with a scraper.

A selection of nursery rhyme and children's book characters have been combined to form a wall painting which would charm any child. The architectural features of the room have been taken very much into account when planning the design, which gives it an extra personalized effect. A trompe l'oeil effect (i.e., something intended to deceive the eye) has been created by the pretend skylight through which various favourite characters are visible. Not only is this a very clever effect, but it also gives the feeling that the room has been 'opened out', making it appear more spacious. There has been tremendous attention to detail in the painting (which has been carried out using acrylic paint) and, most importantly, there is a sense that the person who carried the work out was really enjoying themselves.

Relief wallcoverings bring pattern and interest to walls, inexpensively and without dominating. Since you must paint the paper once it is hung you can also choose any colour you like (mix-while-you-wait ranges offer an almost infinite choice of tones) to fit in with the other furnishings, and should you wish to change the colour you can repaint over the paper several times before it will need replacing. The paint gives a tough finish to the walls (you can use emulsion — or eggshell if you want extra toughness), and you also have the insulating qualities provided by the paper, making the walls feel warm to touch.

You can also, as here, pick out parts of the design in contrasting paint — older children may enjoy doing this (be sure to supervise closely). Should they make a mess, it is a simple job to paint over it with the background colour! This picture also shows how second-hand furniture can be made to look stunning with just a coat of paint. This schoolroom chair, desk and shelving unit have been painted with blue gloss paint and look as good as new, and very stylish. Also, a magnetic 'blackboard' has been created by painting an old metal tray green and hanging it on the wall.

When you reach a sound edge, blend the edges together using wet or dry paper. If the walls are still powdery and dusty, give them a coat of stabilizing solution after doing any necessary filling. If paint is in such bad condition that it needs stripping completely, the easiest method is to use a hot-air paint stripper. (This may not, however, be suitable for use on metalwork. Check with the manufacturer of the stripper if necessary.) A hot-air gun is suitable for use on emulsion or oil-based paint. It melts the paint and brings it up in blisters which can then be scraped away with a scraper. A shave-hook can be used to remove paint caught in mouldings or cracks. The gun should be kept moving so that the surface does not become scorched, and always work from bottom to top. Do not let the hot scrapings fall on your skin or you can get a nasty burn. If you are stripping windows, protect the panes of glass with hardboard or something similar, otherwise the heat will break the glass. Special accessories are also available for hot air guns which make stripping windows easier. Once you have removed all the old paint, wash it over with a mild washing-up liquid solution, then sand down and dust over. Allow to dry out thoroughly before repainting.

Cracks or holes in plasterwork or chips out of woodwork must be filled and sanded level before you can paint over them. The cheapest filler for walls is cellulose powder which is mixed with water before use. Flexible, ready-mixed filler is best for wood and for cracks where surfaces join. It is also much more convenient for repairing small amounts of cracking and holes in walls but it works out more expensive than powdered filler. Small cracks may need opening up, using a screwdriver, stripping knife or filling knife, in order to allow the filler a proper grip (A). Remove any dust with an old toothbrush or small paintbrush (B). Pack in the filler using a small filling knife (C). Allow to dry before sanding smooth (D). Larger holes should be cut back to sound plaster, well brushed out and then filled with thin layers of filler, allowing each one to dry before adding the next, until the filler stands slightly higher than the surrounding surface. Once dry, sand the surface down so it is flush with the wall. If a hole is bigger than about 20 cm (8 in) in diameter, do not try to tackle it yourself. Call in a plasterer.

Finally any walls, paintwork or radiators that have previously been painted with an oil-based paint should be lightly rubbed down with wet and dry paper to give a 'key' for the next paint. Wash the surfaces as described for paintwork in good condition above.

Painting Order

Tackle painting in this order:

1 Ceilings — these are the highest point, so to avoid drips landing on finished paintwork, paint them first.
2 Walls — work away from the light, top to bottom. If you are wallpapering leave out this stage and hang the paper last.
3 Woodwork — window frames, picture rail and then doors.
4 Radiators.
5 Skirting boards.

How much paint should you buy?

Work out the amount of each shade of paint required as follows:

1 Measure the width of one of the walls, in metres.
2 Measure the height of the wall.
3 Multiply these two numbers together — make a note of the result.
4 Repeat steps 1 to 3 for any other walls of the same shade.
5 Add together all the numbers obtained in step 4. This gives you the total area in square metres for this particular shade.
6 Divide the number you have obtained by the figure given (for coverage in square metres per litre of paint) on the individual can of paint you are using. The following table is a general guide to these amounts:

Type of paint	Approximate area covered*
Primer	5–16
Undercoat	15–17
Non-drip gloss	12–15
Liquid gloss	17
Eggshell	16
Matt vinyl/vinyl matt emulsion	12–15
Silk vinyl/vinyl silk emulsion	11–14
Solid roller emulsion	11–13

square metres per litre of paint

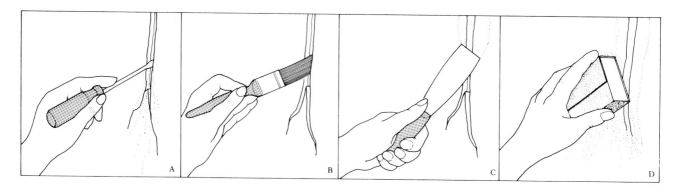

7 The result is the number of litres of that particular shade that you will need to buy, *per coat*. Round up to the nearest litre, and buy sufficient for the number of coats that you will need (see paint chart).

8 Repeat steps 1 to 7 for any other shade(s) that you are using.

9 For ceilings, measure the width and the length, and then carry on from step 3.

10 Small areas of woodwork are more difficult to estimate, because of the complicated shapes involved, but generally you will need much less than for walls. Add up all the lengths of wood to be painted. The following list shows you approximately how much length of each particular item will make up one square metre:

Window frames	10–13 metres
Window sills	6
Glazing bars	16
Shallow skirting	10
Deep skirting	3–6

Add all the amounts together, and follow steps 6–8, above.

How to paint

○ Before you open the tin of paint, read the instructions on it carefully. Once it is open, paint may drip down the side and obscure the writing.

○ Gel paints (non-drip) should not be stirred as this turns them to liquid and they will then drip. All other types of paint should be stirred with a broad bladed piece of wood such as an old ruler.

○ Decant your paint into a paint kettle before you start work. This is a small plastic or metal bucket, available from hardware stores. It stops stray bristles and dirt getting into the can and is much safer to manage up a ladder. S-shaped hooks are available to hang the kettle on the rungs. Only fill the kettle so that paint comes half-way up the bristles of your brush. Dipping it in any further will

make the brush hard to clean.

○ During breaks and after cleaning, wrap brushes in foil or kitchen film. Always clean equipment carefully after use.

Choosing brushes and rollers

A roller is the best way to put on emulsion. Solid emulsion which is non-drip and comes complete with its own tray, makes things even simpler. Choose a short pile mohair sleeve for eggshell, vinyl silk emulsion and solid emulsion paint and a lambswool sleeve for vinyl matt emulsion. Do not buy the widest roller because you think it will speed things up, it may be too heavy to use comfortably. Make sure that the roller and tray you choose are compatible sizes.

The best brushes have the longest, densest and most springy bristles. Natural hog bristle is best. You basically only need four brushes to cover most jobs: 12 mm (½ in) and 2.5 cm (1 in) are suitable for windows, 5 cm (2 in) for skirtings and doors, and 10 cm (4 in) for walls and ceilings. A 1.9 cm (¾ in) cutting-in brush with sloping bristles is also useful for windows and skirting.

Rinse new brushes through first in water and flex them against the palm of your hand to get rid of as many loose bristles as possible.

APPLYING THE PAINT

1 **Painting with a Brush** Unless you are using a gel paint (which must not be stirred), stir the paint thoroughly with a broad-bladed stick such as an old ruler. Transfer enough to half-fill the paint kettle. Make sure the brush is free of dirt and loose bristles. Dip the brush into the paint, to a depth of about one third of the length of the bristles, and wipe off excess paint on the side of the kettle. Hold the brush with your thumb on one side of the metal ferrule, and your fingers on the other, so that the handle nestles between your thumb and first finger. Put the paint on with straight parallel strokes, and then at right angles to spread the paint. Solvent-based paint should be finished off with light strokes in one direction to avoid brush marks.

2 **Painting with a Roller** After stirring the paint, pour some into the tray to about halfway up the slope. Dip the roller into the paint, and gently roll it backwards and forwards on the slope of the tray to distribute the paint evenly. Apply the paint using zig-zag strokes, until the surface is well covered. Finish off solvent-based paint with strokes in one direction.

3 **Ceilings** Start painting in a corner at the window end of the room. Work across the ceiling in a strip about 60 cm (2 ft) wide.

Start the second strip from the same side as the first, to ensure that the edge of the previous strip is still wet, and will accept the new paint. Carry on until the whole ceiling is covered. If using a roller, start by painting the edges and corners that the roller won't reach with a cutting-in brush. It is important to finish the whole ceiling without stopping, as you will get brush marks if you paint over a dry area. If there is a ceiling rose, then **switch off the electricity at the mains**, unscrew the rose cover, and paint up to the backplate with a small brush. When the whole surface is completely dry, apply a second coat in the same way as the first, keeping any overlaps in a different place where possible, so as to avoid a paint build-up.

4 **Walls** Start at the top corner of a wall, near a window. Paint in horizontal strips when using emulsion, vertical strips with solvent-based. Start each strip from the same side as the preceding one (as for ceilings), and pay particular attention to blending the joins between the strips. Use a cutting-in brush to accurately paint the top and bottom edges of the walls, and around door and window frames, and skirtings. Cut in the edges first if using a roller, before applying paint to the main

area. When encountering electrical sockets, switches, etc., **switch off at the mains,** then loosen the screws holding the mounting box or face plate, and paint behind it.

5 **Doors** Remove the door handle and any other fittings, and hold the door open with a wedge. If it is a flush door then start painting from the top, and work down in strips, finishing off as you go with light vertical strokes. Carefully blend adjoining strips. When the main area is finished, paint the door edges with a small brush. If the door has panels, then these should be painted first, working from the edge of the panels to the centre. Next paint the horizontal and vertical sections of the door, again blending carefully, and then paint the edges. Finally paint the architrave, using a cutting-in brush where the wood adjoins the wall.

6 **Windows** It is best to paint windows in the morning, so that they will be dry enough to close again in the evening. Cover all the edges of the glass with masking tape, leaving a small gap so that the paint will cover the putty and seal onto the very edge of the glass. Paint the inner sections of wood first, using a cutting-in brush where necessary, and continue with the outer sections, then the edges, and lastly the frame. When the paint is touch-dry (but not before), carefully remove the masking tape, and use a scraper to remove any paint which may have splashed on the glass. When working with casement windows, leave the stay until last so that you can use to adjust the window without getting paint on your hands. If you have sash windows then paint the outer sash first, sliding the windows as necessary to reach all parts, and then paint the inner sash. Finally paint the runners (keeping the paint clear of the sash cords), and the frame. Insert some matchsticks between the frame and the sashes to prevent sticking.

7 **Radiators** If you are using ordinary solvent-based paint, turn the heating off, and allow the radiators to cool. Paint the front of the radiator, ending with strokes in one direction to make a smooth finish. The back of the radiator is easier to tackle if you have a long-handled radiator brush. There may still be some areas that are difficult to reach, but if they can't be seen, they don't need to be covered. Take care not to get any paint on valves, or joints that may need to be undone. Paint pipework along its length, and hold a piece of card between the wall and the pipe where necessary to avoid getting paint on the wall. If you are using special radiator paint, then follow the manufacturer's instructions.

8 **Skirtings** Use a cutting-in brush to paint the edge of the skirting board where it meets the wall. Use a larger brush for the main area of the board, and it is helpful to have a paint shield (a piece of card will do) to keep paint off the floor. Press the shield into the corner between the floor and the skirting, and move it along the floor as you paint each section, wiping the shield clean of paint each time. If there is a carpet, then either remove it, or use the paint shield and the cutting-in brush to reduce the risk of getting paint on the carpet.

9 **Cleaning-up** It is important to clean equipment carefully after use. Scrape solvent-based paint off brushes with the back of an old knife, on to newspaper. Wash out the brushes in white spirit or brush cleaner, followed by soapy water. Finally rinse in clean water, and allow to dry. Water-based paint can be washed off by holding the brushes under the cold tap, and splaying the bristles with your fingers so that the water can wash the paint away. Store any left-over paint in screw-top jars, keeping it fresh for any touching-up that will (inevitably!) be needed.

PAINT EFFECTS FOR WALLS

Plain painted walls can sometimes look rather monotonous so paint effects were developed centuries ago to make plain walls look more interesting and to break up the surface. Paint effects can also make a good background for stencilling and the effect is particularly subtle when you use some of the same colours for both. Paint effects also enable you to match the wall colours to the colours of the other furnishings, and also to disguise uneven walls, although the surface must be basically sound — nothing will disguise peeling plaster.

Children's rooms are often small so there is not a huge area to cover and so they provide a good place to experiment, especially as small children will not be fussy if there are a few mistakes. Anyway, paint effects are meant to look hand-done so the effect does not have to be perfect. It is the overall appearance that is important, not close-up detail.

Some techniques are more difficult than others, but the easiest ones can be carried out with emulsion or eggshell paint. Experts use oil-based glazes which have to be mixed up specially. However, it is possible to get very good effects just by using ordinary paint. Remember, if you wish to continue the effect across wood and metal work (and these effects are very good ways of disguising pipes, radiators and fitted cupboards) then you will have to switch to solvent-based paint, preferably eggshell, for these surfaces.

For preparing the walls for paint effects, see pages 17–20.

General hints

○ Protect areas around your work with newspaper and masking tape, dust sheets and/or plastic sheeting.
○ Wear rubber gloves.
○ All paint effects require a base coat which, for the effects described here should be vinyl matt emulsion for walls and eggshell for wood or metalwork.
○ Always practise effects on a piece of old board or paper first.

If you want to be a traditionalist and have a blue colour scheme for a baby boy, then choose a sunny, south-facing room, otherwise the effect will be cold and lacking in comfort. If the room is north-facing opt for a warmer colour, such as yellow. You may, of course, decide you like blue anyway, whether it's going to be a boy or a girl. Blue, however, being a cool colour, has the advantage of making small rooms look larger, because cool colours tend to look as though they are receding.

A teddy-bear and rocking-horse frieze has been stencilled at dado height — an ideal position because it can easily be seen by a small child. As it is a stencilled, and not a wall-paper frieze it cannot be picked off the wall by little fingers. It is important, when planning the height of a frieze, to check that the height you have chosen is suitable all the way around the

room. It is easy to make the mistake of deciding the height by looking at just one wall and then finding, once you start stencilling, that it comes to an inconvenient position on another wall. Here, the height of the work-top on the built-in unit was the fixture that decided the position of the stencilling.

Consider what you are going to do with the large, blank areas of wall when you plan the scheme. Here a delightful Victorian name picture gives impact to the alcove while bold, cheerful balloon shapes create a focal point in the corner. Simple shapes have been stencilled with a shaded effect, to make the balloons look rounded. The balloon motif has been repeated on the end of the cot, as has the teddy from the frieze, to give a co-ordinated look. A clown mobile has been positioned within the baby's line of vision, but high enough to prevent

it being reached and pulled down.

Fitted furniture makes the best use of space, keeping the floor uncluttered to give more room for playing, and also to make cleaning easier. Adult-sized storage makes more sense than cute baby furniture which will soon be out-grown. A fitted unit provides a useful storage and changing area — later it can be transformed into a dressing table or used as a desk for homework. White, natural woods or a surface that can be painted are good finishes for fitted furniture, as they will go with almost any room scheme and, at a future date, a simple change of handles will give a whole new look.

PVC-coated cork tiles make a very sensible and durable choice for the floor which is given extra colour and interest in the form of an embroidered felt rug. When laid on a smooth floor, rugs should always be used with a non-slip backing.

○ Switch electricity off at the mains when working round switches and power points.

○ Leave each coat to dry before you go on to the next.

○ As long as you use the right paint for the surface there is no need to varnish over the top of most paint effects.

○ Clean brushes and equipment carefully as soon as you have finished.

Sponging

Sponging is one of the simplest and subtlest effects and makes a good starting point for the beginner.

You will need

A large natural sea sponge (available from chemists and specialist painting shops)
A paint roller tray
A piece of flat scrap material for practice
Emulsion base-coat, plus two or three closely related top coat colours for walls; use eggshell for wood or metalwork

1 Paint walls using the base-coat colour and allow to dry. Dampen the sponge (with water if you are using emulsion and white spirit if you are using solvent-based paint) and squeeze it out well to make it more pliable. It is important to use a natural sponge, not a synthetic or cellulose one. Pour one of the top-coat colours into a paint roller tray, thin slightly using water for emulsion and white spirit for solvent-

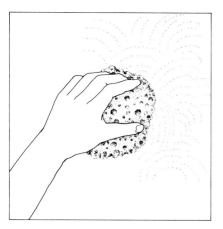

based paint, then dip your sponge into it lightly and remove the excess on the grooved slope. Blot on a scrap piece of board to check you have the right amount of paint. Repeat this each time you load up the sponge.

2 Work from the top of the wall downwards. Dab the sponge on the wall gently at random, moving the sponge so the pattern does not become regular, and working evenly to build up the pattern. Keep moving randomly over a wide area because each time you load up the sponge the first few dabs will be darker. Make sure the colour does not build-up at corners or by doors, windows and skirtings. To avoid this, leave the edges of the wall until last then fill in later with the corner of a sponge. Aim to keep the colour distribution even. Rinse out the sponge with water or white spirit now and again, depending on the type of paint you are using, to prevent it becoming clogged up.

3 Carry on until the whole wall is mottled with sponging, you should still be able to see quite a large amount of background colour.

4 Wait until one colour is dry before starting the next. Work from the top as before and blend all the colours, but leave some of the background showing. Stand back. If the effect is not subtle enough sponge over lightly with the background colour to soften the effect.

Colour washing

Colour washing gives a delightfully soft and subtle effect for walls and its delicacy makes it particularly suitable for the nursery. This effect is only suitable for walls, not radiators, pipes or woodwork.

You will need

Matt emulsion for the base coat (white or a pale colour) and top coat (a stronger version of the first colour)
A roller or brush for the base coat
One 5 cm (2 in) and one 10 cm (4 in) wall brush for colour washing

Paint roller tray
Clear emulsion glaze (available from specialist paint shops)

1 Cover the wall with a coat of full-strength emulsion. Then dilute the slightly stronger colour with three parts water to one part paint.

2 Using a 5 cm (2 in) wall brush, apply the first coat. Move the brush randomly so that some areas have more paint on than others, making sure you leave some areas of the background uncovered. Brush on in loose, bold strokes that leave the brushmarks visible. Beware of runs and avoid a build-up of paint, especially at corners and at skirting level.

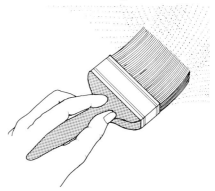

3 When the first coat has dried, apply the second. Dilute the paint as before and apply with a 10 cm (4 in) wall brush, covering the whole wall area this time. Again, brush the paint in a random, criss-cross movement.

4 To make this finish more durable, give it a coat of clear emulsion glaze once the last coat has dried.

Stippling

Stippling is a subtle effect, a bit like sponging, which is usually done with a special stippling brush (available from specialist paint effect shops). However, these brushes are fairly pricey so if you want to have a go without spending money on a special brush you can always experiment with a household sweeping brush, a shoe brush or a flat bottomed scrubbing brush. Opt for natural, rather than plastic or nylon, bristles.

You will need

Matt emulsion for the base coat, plus two or more emulsion colours for stippling, you will need to use eggshell for metalwork and woodwork

A brush or roller to apply the base coat

Specialist stippling brush or substitute (see above)

Paint roller tray

1 Paint the base coat and allow to dry. Pour a small amount of your first topcoat colour into the tray and dab the dry stipple brush onto it. Do not pick up too much or you may clog the bristles. Test it out on a piece of scrap material first. If the paint seems a bit thick, thin it a little (use water for emulsion and white spirit for eggshell).

2 Once you have the paint consistency right, dab the brush on the wall with a gentle 'pecking' motion. Remember to remove the excess on scrap material each time you load up the brush. Keep moving randomly over a wide area because each time you load up the brush the first few dabs will be darker.

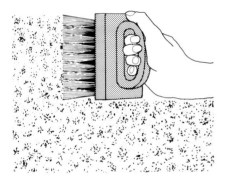

3 When the first top coat is dry apply the second, following the instructions for the first coat but using lighter pressure. After each use clean your stippling brush following the instructions on page 22, then dry on kitchen paper.

Splattering

Splattering gives a wonderfully random and casual effect and looks especially effective if you use several colours together. It does,

however, make rather a mess, so make sure you protect all surfaces that you do not want splattering with plastic sheeting or thick layers of newspaper held in place with masking tape. You can use this effect on walls, metalwork and woodwork.

You will need

A matt emulsion base coat, plus at least two other emulsion colours for walls; use eggshell for wood or metalwork

Roller or brush for base coat

A wide paintbrush for splattering

An old cake cooling rack or similar grid

Plastic sheeting or newspaper and masking tape

1 Paint the base colour and leave to dry.

2 Dip a wide brush in your splattering colour, remove the excess paint on a clean scrap surface such as an old piece of board, then hold the grid about 20 cm (8 in) from

the wall and run the brush carefully across the grid. Repeat each time you reload the brush.

3 Splatter on the second colour when the first one is dry. Allow that to dry and add any further colours, waiting for each to dry before you proceed.

STENCILLING ON WALLS AND DOORS

Stencilling brings pattern, character and interest to plain walls and doors, as well as being fun to do, and stencils look particularly effective when used in conjunction with paint effects. You can either buy pre-cut designs or make your own. There are several companies who specialize in pre-cut stencils and they usually offer a mail-order service. They also supply other special equipment for stencilling.

Making your own stencils

Although there is a wide range of excellent ready-cut stencils for children's rooms, you may like to have a go at creating your own designs. You can take a design from fabric, wallpaper or bed linen, or you can devise motifs from children's books, wrapping paper, greetings cards, folk art, or anything else that takes your fancy. You can also use

children's drawings and paintings, or make up designs youself. If you choose to make your own designs, acetate or Mylar is best for the stencil itself because it is flexible and also transparent, so you can see what you are doing more easily.

Choosing paint

The type of paint you need to use for your stencilling will depend on the type of surface you are working on. Ideally, walls should have been painted with matt emulsion, woodwork and metalwork should have been painted with eggshell.

Specialist stencil paints are available from stencilling shops which can be used on various surfaces. These are quick-drying but are available in a small range of colours (although you can mix them) and work out fairly expensive for large areas. These paints

should be applied following manufacturer's instructions, and check they are suitable for your intended surface before buying.

Walls painted with matt emulsion can also be stencilled using more of the same paint, plus a piece of sponge or a special stencilling brush (some people swear by one or the other!). Solvent-based paints can be stencilled on using spray paint (observe safety instructions carefully), artists' acrylics, or eggshell paint — but this last is slow drying and can be messy. Spray paints and acrylics are also suitable for use on emulsion-painted walls.

You will need

Suitable paint
White spirit to clean up if you are using solvent-based paints
Paper
Acetate or Mylar (from art shops)
Spirit marker (from art shops)
Scalpel or craft knife (from art shops)
Self-healing cutting board, optional (from art shops)
Spray glue, optional (from art shops)

A plain cream wall gets a very charming finishing touch in the form of this ready-cut cat stencil. The frieze is at the best height for a child to enjoy it and has been stencilled using emulsion paint. The motif has been repeated on the chest of drawers, which had already been painted with eggshell.

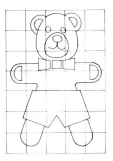

Enlarging a motif by squaring up

Low-tack masking tape (from art shops)
If you are not using spray paint:
Paint roller tray, or other similar container
Synthetic bath sponge cut into large chunks or stencil brush to apply paint. If using special stencil paints follow manufacturer's instructions for how to apply.

○ Decide whether you want a border or a randomly spaced design, and decide where it is to go in the room
○ If you have recently painted the surface that you are going to stencil, make sure it is completely dry before you start.
○ If you are stencilling on gloss paint you will need to key the surface slightly with fine wet-and-dry paper first.
○ Wear rubber gloves.
○ Practise on scrap material first.

1 Draw or trace your motif onto a sheet of paper, enlarging it if necessary, so that it

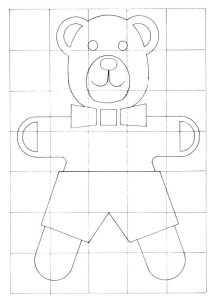

is the actual size of the proposed stencil. The easiest way to enlarge is on an enlarging photocopier or, failing that, by squaring up. To square up, draw a grid over the motif. If you want the finished image to be twice as big, for example, draw another grid with the squares twice as large and copy the details from each square on the small grid on to the larger one. If your design is a border or frieze, draw a guideline on the paper above or below and parallel to the design. This line will be copied on to each stencil and used as a guide for stencilling on the wall.

Teddy frieze

GUIDE LINE

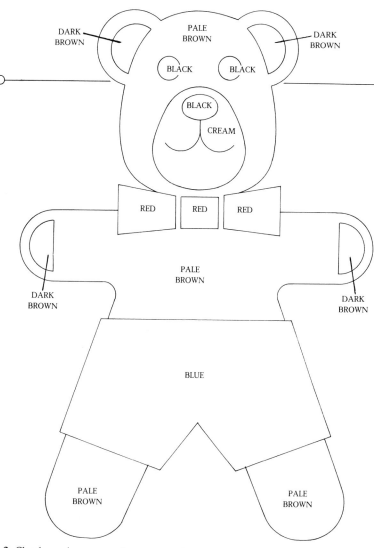

DARK BROWN

PALE BROWN

DARK BROWN

BLACK BLACK

BLACK

CREAM

RED RED RED

DARK BROWN

PALE BROWN

DARK BROWN

BLUE

PALE BROWN

PALE BROWN

design is a frieze, also trace the guideline on to each stencil.

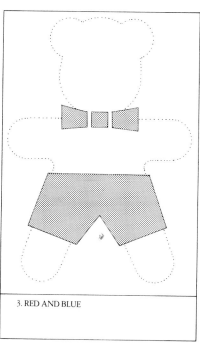

3. RED AND BLUE

2 Clearly mark any areas that you want in different colours.

3 You will need one sheet of acetate for each colour, although, if two or more colours are widely spaced apart, you can put them together on the same stencil. Make sure the sheets are at least 10 cm

(4 in) larger all round than the motif. This gives a margin to prevent paint accidentally getting on to the surrounding surface once you start stencilling. Lay the sheets over the drawing and, using a spirit-based marking pen, trace off all the outlines on to each sheet. If the

4 Write the name of the colour on each sheet (or more than one name if you are combining colours on a sheet) and carefully cut out the parts of the design on each sheet that you wish to appear in that particular colour. For best results use a scalpel and self-healing cutting board. Any pen lines left that you have not cut on will help you to position the colours on top of each other when you come to stencil. If you are stencilling a

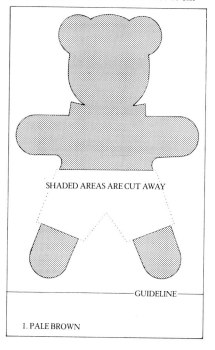

SHADED AREAS ARE CUT AWAY

GUIDELINE

1. PALE BROWN

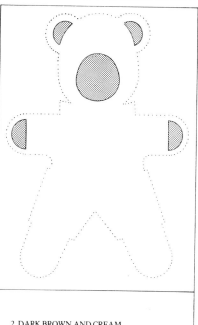

2. DARK BROWN AND CREAM

4. BLACK

frieze, also mark on the stencil where the next motifs come at both ends of the stencil. This helps you to line the design up accurately when you come to stencil the repeat.

5 Decide exactly where you want the stencil to go, centre it on the wall or door using a measure if necessary. If you are stencilling a frieze, position the stencil on the wall in the correct position and mark the position of the guideline. Continue this line across the wall, parallel to the floor or ceiling by stretching cotton thread and holding it in place with dots of low-tack masking tape. This will be the line against which you position the guideline on each stencil.

6 Start with the stencil that covers the largest area and/or that has other colours on top of it. Working in a well ventilated area, spray very lightly over the back of the stencil with spray glue (this stage is optional) and allow to get tacky. Then place the stencil in position, pressing it lightly all over if you have spray-glued it. Whether or not you have glued it, stick the stencil in place with low-tack masking tape.

7 Pour out a small amount of your first colour on to a paint roller tray or other suitable container. If the paint is very thick, thin with a little water (for emulsion) or white spirit (for solvent-

based paint). If you are using spray-paint build up the effect using layers of light coats and holding card over the areas you do not want sprayed.

8 Alternatively, if you are using ordinary paint put on a pair of rubber gloves and dip a piece of sponge into the paint and then dab it on to the ribbed part of the paint tray or on to scrap material until the result is a drier, even effect rather than a wet and blobby look.

9 Dab the sponge firmly on to the stencil, repeating step 7 each time you need more paint. Never try to stencil with too much paint, or the effect will be coarse and uneven and paint may seep under the edges of the stencil.

10 Once you have completed the first colour, let it dry (this will take much longer with solvent-based paint than with emulsion). Then, following step 5 again, position the next stencil on top of the last, lining up the outline on the current stencil with the previous piece of stencilling.

11 Clean your paint tray (take a new piece of sponge if necessary — with solvent-based paint this is very likely) and repeat steps 6 and 7 with the next colour.

12 Repeat these stages until you have finished the design.

13 Clean up carefully and allow the paint plenty of time to dry.

Spray paint drifts so be sure to mask off the surrounding area and floor carefully.

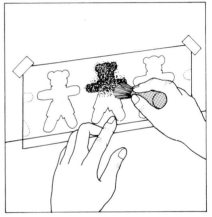

Instead of using a sponge you may prefer a stencil brush so experiment with both.

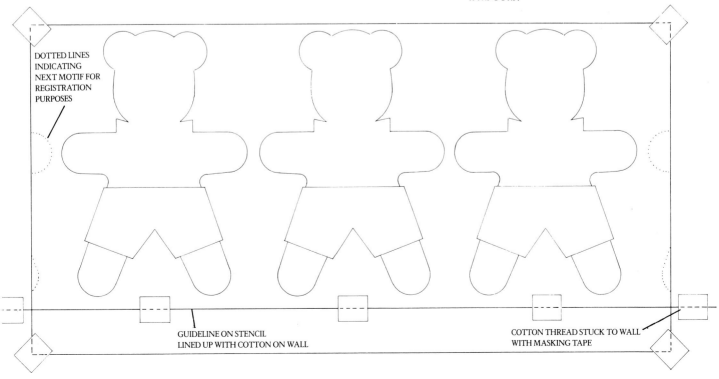

DOTTED LINES INDICATING NEXT MOTIF FOR REGISTRATION PURPOSES

GUIDELINE ON STENCIL LINED UP WITH COTTON ON WALL

COTTON THREAD STUCK TO WALL WITH MASKING TAPE

Painting a blackboard on the wall surrounded by a stencilled frieze

A blackboard on the wall provides an official scribbling area and an outlet for a child's creativity, without using the floor space that would be taken by an easel-type blackboard. You can only paint a blackboard on a painted wall, it is not possible to paint one on wallpaper.

You will need

Wet and dry paper
Blackboard paint
Low-tack masking tape (from art shops or specialist paint effect shops)
A 5 cm (2 in) or 10 cm (4 in) paintbrush, depending on the area you are covering

1 Decide how big you want the blackboard to be and where it is to go.
2 Mark the outline of the blackboard with a straight-edge and pencil, and rub down the area within the lines using wet and dry paper.

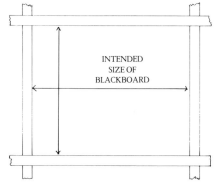

INTENDED
SIZE OF
BLACKBOARD

3 Mask round the edges of the lines with low-tack masking tape.

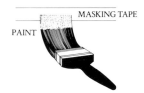

MASKING TAPE
PAINT

4 Paint a coat of blackboard paint within the masked area. When painting up to the masking tape avoid having a heavily loaded brush, and paint inwards over the tape towards the centre of the blackboard. This is to avoid getting paint under the tape. Stick a piece of tape in the central area and experiment first if you like. You can paint your experiments out later!
5 Allow the paint to dry, following manufacturer's instructions.
6 Paint a second and third coat, allowing the paint to dry between each coat.
7 Peel off the masking tape carefully.
8 Stencil a border around the edge, following the instructions given earlier in the chapter for stencilling on walls.

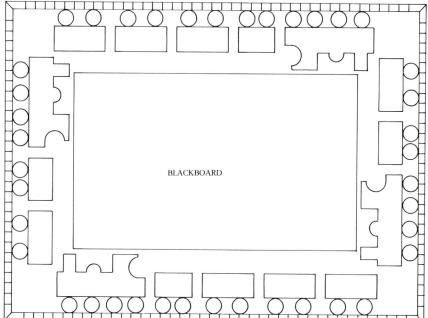

BLACKBOARD

PAINTING MURALS

A child's room is a great place to experiment with freehand painting on the walls, partly because you can be imaginative and experimental, and also because your audience will not be too critical — not until they get much older, anyway. A mural can provide great visual stimulation for a child, create an exciting talking point and can give the illusion of extra space by suggesting openings in the wall.

Before you actually go ahead and start designing a mural, look at the room and decide on the best place for it. Take into account the shape and features of the room to see if these suggest any ideas about the positioning of the mural. It is important to decide where the mural is to begin and end, otherwise it could end up sprawling aimlessly around the room — unless a casual and all-over effect is what you want.

The inspiration for a mural can come from a variety of sources, a children's book

This comic book hero was transferred to the wall by photographing a picture from a book, making a slide from it and projecting the image on to the wall using a slide projector. The image was then traced round and painted using emulsion and acrylic paints. The mural is very dominant in the room and creates a stunning impact. However, you must be sure that your child is keen on the idea too, as some children could find such an image frightening.

illustration, a postcard or birthday card, to designing your own creation from scratch, constructing imaginary landscapes and creatures or painting wild and abstract shapes. Try looking at art books in your local library. Certain artists in particular are worth seeking out, such as Paul Klee, Joan Miro, Wassily Kandinsky, Pablo Picasso, Franz Marc, August Macke, Raoul Dufy and Henri Matisse. Books on folk art, naïve art and tribal art may also provide you with ideas, if you want to do something fairly representational look at children's reference books on animals, plants, aeroplanes, ships, and so on. Do be careful, however, not to design anything which may frighten a child.

You do not need lots of special equipment to paint a mural and some of it you may have already. The wall you paint must be sound and have been prepared for painting as described above. It should then be painted with a background coat or two of vinyl matt emulsion. The type of paint you choose for the mural will depend on how much money you want to spend, the size of the mural, what sort of detail you want.

The recommended type of paints for a mural are artists' acrylics, available from art shops. These are water-based, so brushes are easy to clean (provided you do it straight away), there is no smell, and the paints are quick drying. Any mistakes can also be wiped away, before the paint dries, with a damp cloth or sponge. Acrylics also dry to a nice matt finish, and do not yellow with age. You can also get some very subtle effects by diluting colours and blending colours into each other, so it pays to experiment, and this type of paint is particularly useful for fine detail. However, artists' acrylics are not cheap, and it is a fairly expensive proposition to buy enough paint to cover a whole wall. Check that all the colours you buy are non-toxic as some acrylic colours are poisonous.

A cheaper alternative is vinyl or PVA paint, also from art shops. These are not so sophisticated as artists' acrylics and do not come in such good colours, but you may find they are adequate for what you want. The cheapest choice is matt emulsion: this is particularly good for large areas of flat colour

and comes in a fantastically wide range of colours, especially if you opt for mix-to-order ranges. Tester pots are a very cheap way of buying small quantities of colour. You can also tint emulsion with artists' acrylics if you wish. A mural painted with emulsion will not last for ever, but it will certainly be durable enough to provide enjoyment throughout at least one childhood.

You may wish to extend your mural over gloss paint or eggshell. You will need to rub it down with wet and dry paper or liquid sander, to provide a good key for the paint; eggshell will only need a light rub down. You can then use artists' acrylic or PVA.

You will also need brushes, and again the sizes you will need depend on the size and detail of your mural. For covering large areas, use good quality household brushes. The sizes 2.5 cm (1 in), 4 cm (1½ in), 5 cm (2 in) and 10 cm (4 in) should be adequate for most purposes. For finer detail you will need artists' brushes. Buy a selection of cheap oil-painting brushes and nylon watercolour brushes.

You will need

Paper
Low-tack masking tape
Paint (see above)
Selection of brushes (see above)

1 Prepare the wall for painting as described above.

2 Once you have decided on your design, draw or paint a small-scale version on a

piece of paper (or whatever way you like to work — use crayons or sticky coloured paper if you prefer).

3 Square up the design by drawing a grid over it (or trace it on to tracing paper and draw a grid on that). For instructions see 'stencilling on walls' on page 25. The size of the squares will depend on the detail of your drawing, but if your original drawing was on an A4 sheet of paper, for example, a 2.5 cm (1 in) grid would be about right.

4 Mark out an enlarged grid on the wall, in exactly the same proportions, the size you want the finished mural. You can do this with chalk, very light pencil or you can tape pieces of cotton thread on the wall with low-tack masking tape. Then transfer the small drawing to the big grid by copying what is in each small square to its related big square.

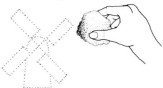

5 Alternatively you can draw the design out full size on a large sheet of paper (taping pieces together if necessary). Prick round the outlines with a pin, stick the paper in position on the wall, and rub over the lines with cotton wool dipped in powdered charcoal. Remove the paper carefully, to avoid smudging, and join up the dots lightly with a soft pencil (another method

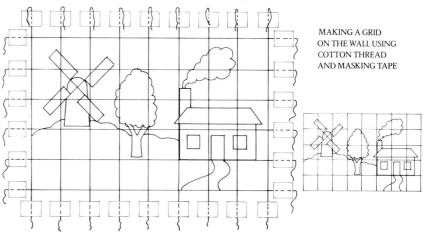

MAKING A GRID
ON THE WALL USING
COTTON THREAD
AND MASKING TAPE

Idea for mural

is to use a slide projector — see below). Make any pencil drawing as light as possible because pencil has a way of showing through paint.

6 Paint out the design using emulsion for large areas and acrylic or PVA paint for finer detail. There is no need to varnish the mural unless you think it is going to get particularly heavy wear, in which case you can use a clear emulsion glaze, which is less likely to yellow than oil-based varnish.

Creating a mural using a slide projector

A slide projector makes it easy to transfer an image on to a wall. You can either use an existing transparency or transparencies, such as a picture of a funfair, aeroplane, zoo animals or model village, for example, or you

can buy transparencies. Art galleries and museums often sell transparencies of their exhibits and some may be suitable images for murals, or you can take a picture specially from a book, card or comic. A clear black and white image works best for this method, such as those in painting books and comic strips. Set up the camera so that the image almost fills the frame. If you are unable to photograph it yourself, a photographic shop or laboratory may be able to do it for you.

You will need

A camera capable of focusing close-up
Slide film
Projector capable of projecting your size of slide
A 'B' pencil
Emulsion and/or acrylic paints
Various sizes of artists' brushes

1 Prepare the wall as described above, and paint it with the background colour in matt vinyl emulsion.

2 Darken the room and project the picture on to the wall. Move the projector backwards and forwards and adjust the focusing until the picture is the exact size you want and in the correct position.

3 Trace the outlines on to the wall carefully. Because the picture is enlarged the outlines may appear considerably thicker, so indicate this in your tracing if you think they will add to the effect.

5 Check that the slide is not becoming too hot. Turn the projector off from time to time to allow the slide to cool down.

6 Switch off the projector, open the curtains or turn on the light and paint the design using emulsion and/or acrylic or PVA paints.

Paint Summary Chart

Stage of work or product	Notes	Average coverage per litre	Recoatable in about…	Types of surface					
				Bare wood	Old, sound paint on wood	Old, unsound paint on wood	Metal and Radiators	Bare plaster	Previously papered or painted walls & ceilings
Preparation	Very important stage — must be done carefully	—	—	Fill holes, rub down, wipe over, use knotting if necessary	Wash down, rub down, wipe over	Scrape or strip off, rub down, treat as bare wood	If unpainted, remove grease and oil with white spirit, if painted, prepare as for painted wood	Surface must be clean and dry, new plaster must be dry	Remove any wallpaper unless painting over lining paper or anaglypta, otherwise wash, fill, scrape off any flaking paint, rub down & wipe over
Primer	Only needed for bare or loose surfaces, use a general purpose or specialist product, make sure it is non-toxic	5–16 sq m depending on type & on surface	2–24 hrs depending on type	Wood primer or universal primer	Not needed	As for bare wood	Universal primer or metal primer, only needed for bare surfaces	Primer/sealer or one coat of thinned emulsion	If paint has been removed, treat as for bare plaster, if wall is still powdery, treat with stabilising solution, otherwise primer not needed
Undercoat	A preparatory coat for solvent based paints only, i.e. gloss or eggshell; not needed for one-coat paints	15–17 sq m	16 hrs	Only needed if you are using liquid gloss	Only needed if you are changing colour	As for bare wood	Only needed if you are using liquid gloss, but do not use on radiators or hot pipes	Not needed	Only needed if changing colour and using eggshell
Non drip gloss	Tough gloss finish, easy to use	12–15 sq m	16 hrs	1–2 coats	1–2 coats	1–2 coats	1–2 coats	Not really suitable	Not really suitable
Liquid gloss	Tough high gloss finish, needs skill	17 sq m	16 hrs	1–2 coats	1–2 coats	1–2 coats	1–2 coats	Not really suitable	Not really suitable
Eggshell	Harwearing finish with a gentle sheen, not quite as tough or easy to clean as gloss	16 sq m	16 hrs	1–2 coats	1–2 coats	1–2 coats	1–2 coats	Can be used where an extra tough finish is needed, 1–2 coats	Can be used where an extra tough finish is needed, 1–2 coats
Matt vinyl/vinyl matt emulsion	Hardwearing, matt finish, not quite as easy to clean as vinyl silk	12–15 sq m	6 hrs	Not suitable	Not suitable	Not suitable	Not suitable	1–2 coats	1–2 coats
Silk vinyl/vinyl silk emulsion	Hardwearing, washable silk finish	11–14 sq m	6 hrs	Not suitable	Not suitable	Not suitable	Not suitable	1–2 coats	1–2 coats
Solid roller emulsion	Available in matt & silk finishes in a limited colour range, non-drip, very easy to use with a roller	11–13 sq m	6 hrs	Not suitable	Not suitable	Not suitable	Not suitable	1–2 coats	1–2 coats

A strongly patterned wallpaper such as this can create a strong impact in a child's room, especially when combined with such wonderfully vibrant paintwork. The positioning of the border, at skirting height, makes an unusual but highly effective choice, especially as children tend to play on the floor anyway. The moulding dividing the border from the rest of the paper makes this part of the wall even more of a feature.

The panels of moulding on the door (moulding can be nailed easily on to an ordinary flush door to create this effect) have been filled with rectangles of the wallpaper which turns an ordinary door into something special. This room also demonstrates how much difference it makes when you get the details right. The doorhandle, coat hook and light switch in a colour taken from the wallpaper, and which contrasts well with the paintwork, are an important extra dimension.

Remember though, that a wallcovering that dominates the room too much can be rather daunting for a child, as their pictures and personal possessions can begin to look a bit lost. Children will also tire more quickly of decoration that has an obvious character in it, than one that is more abstract in feel. If in doubt, decorate just half the room, or even just one wall and paint the rest of the room in a (pale) co-ordinating colour so your child can display pictures, and other treasures here.

WALLCOVERINGS

It can be a difficult decision whether to paper or paint a child's room. Putting up wallcoverings requires more equipment and skill than painting, although the amount of equipment you will need depends on the type of paper you buy (ready-pasted needs less) and anyway once you have bought the equipment you can use it again and again. From the point of view of the extra skill required, provided you are patient and careful, it is not difficult even for a beginner to make a good job of wallpapering. It is also less messy than painting (splashes of glue are much easier to deal with than splashes of paint) and it does not smell or give off fumes in the way that paint does.

Wallcoverings also have the advantage of hiding imperfections in walls better than paint, particularly if the pattern is strong. Children's wallcoverings are often produced with co-ordinating fabrics, which makes easy work of colour scheming!

There is a wide range of specialist designs for children, featuring their favourite characters, and children's wallcoverings offer instant colour, pattern and interest. One important thing to bear in mind is how often you intend redecorating. If you, or your child, choose a design which is very up-to-the minute and the latest craze he may very quickly tire of it. Remember that very babyish designs will be outgrown quickly. But if you do not mind redecorating at frequent intervals, this should pose no problems.

Other considerations when deciding between paper and paint for a child's room are that papering a room tends to work out more expensive than painting it, paper can be peeled off or damaged by little fingers and is more difficult to patch up than paint (it always pays to keep a spare roll) and wallpaper also offers less creative possibilities. Wallpaper can, however be used on doors, and looks particularly effective set into panels, including furniture such as wardrobe doors.

The effects of patterns

Do remember that strongly patterned wallcoverings will make a room appear smaller and will also compete with any pictures on the walls. A small room will look bigger if you choose a small-scale print on a pale background. This type of pattern helps disguise the irregularity of odd-shaped rooms. If the ceiling is sloped, it is a good idea to paper that too, as this will make the room appear more regular. If a room has a low ceiling, vertical stripes will make the walls look taller. But avoid using stripes or strong geometric designs in a room with uneven walls, as any flaws will be exaggerated. Match fabric with the wallcovering to give a more spacious look to a room, this works particularly well if the pattern is small scale.

Which paper to choose?

As well as choosing the right pattern for your child's room, it is very important that the wallcovering should be up to the job from a practical point of view. Although we still often refer to 'wallpaper' nowadays not all wallcoverings are made from paper. For children's rooms, where heavy demands are likely to be made on walls, it is best to invest in a coated or vinyl wallcovering. Wallcoverings specifically designed for children are likely to have a suitable tough finish, provided they are manufactured by a reliable company, but always double check when you buy.

'Standard wallpaper' is, for this reason, unsuitable for children's rooms. It is the old-fashioned type of wallpaper and, unlike other types of wallcovering, has no protective coating. It will not take a lot of wear and gets dirty very easily. In particular do not be tempted to buy cheap versions as a stop-gap. They are often very flimsy and difficult to hang since, once wet with paste, they are likely to tear.

Coated papers have a special protective surface so that water-based stains can be wiped off with a damp cloth or sponge.

Spongeable is the least durable type, then comes washable; super washable is tougher still, and scrubbable paper is durable enough to be cleaned with a soft brush. Obviously, for a child's room, the tougher the finish the better.

These types of paper are often available ready-pasted. You simply soak them in a water trough, supplied with the paper, for a specified amount of time, lift out the paper and stick it straight on the wall. This does away with the need for paste, brushes and pasting tables.

Vinyl wallcoverings are even tougher and more water-resistant than coated papers. They are made from a layer of solid vinyl on a paper backing. Vinyls and washable papers are often dry-peelable, which means you can simply strip the coating off, to leave behind the backing paper which can then be used as lining paper. However, if a child discovers this, you may end up with your paper being stripped off before you intended!

Lining papers

Even if you have decided to paint the walls, rather than paper them, you may consider covering them with lining paper first. Lining paper is a plain white paper which comes in different thicknesses and is used to camouflage unevenness and give a smooth base for wallpaper or paint. If used to paint over it is hung vertically, if it is being used as an 'undercoat' for wallpaper it should be hung horizontally. You should always use the same paste for lining paper as you will be using for the top paper.

'Relief wallcoverings' are white papers with raised patterns which are always painted after hanging, using vinyl silk emulsion, to give a very durable, vinyl finish. (The silk finish makes for easier cleaning and also highlights the pattern better.) Relief wallcoverings also help insulate the room and hide small bumps and imperfections in the wall, especially if you line the walls with lining paper first, but they must still be hung on a sound surface. No paper can cope with damp or peeling walls, so these problems must be seen to before you decorate.

There are several patterns of relief wallcovering specially designed for children and one of the advantages of this type of paper is that the designs are quite subtle while providing surface texture and interest, and so they will not dominate the room. They can also be painted over several times, giving an increasingly tough surface, and any marks or damage can easily be touched over with a lick of paint. Relief wallcoverings also tend to be very reasonably priced, even if you add the cost of the paint to the bill.

If you decide on a wallcovering for your child's room, rather than paint, you will need to measure up and work out how many rolls you need, using this chart. The repeat size of a design affects how much paper you have to buy; the bigger the repeat the more paper you will need as some is wasted in matching up designs. The least wasteful and easiest to hang are free-match or random designs. Make sure that all the rolls you buy carry the same batch number, as different batches can

vary slightly in colour. If in doubt buy an extra roll or two, and it is always useful to keep a spare in case of mishaps. If you find you have overcalculated, many stores will credit you for the extra rolls, provided they still have the same batch in stock.

Wallpaper borders

Wallpaper borders are a quick, inexpensive and easy way to introduce colour and pattern into a room. They are available in lots of jolly children's designs, often to match a co-ordinating wallpaper, though they can also be used on a plain painted wall which is a very economical way to introduce pattern. Simply find a paint colour that matches up to one of the colours in the design, paint the walls with it and add the border.

Borders, used horizontally, make a narrow or high ceilinged room appear wider. They can be used at dado height, just under the ceiling or cornice, at picture rail height, round doors and just above the skirting. The lower down the wall you position one, the better the child will be able to see it. Unfortunately he may also try to peel it off

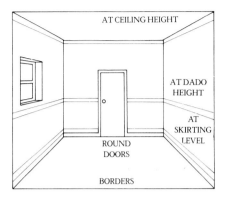

so, again, keep a spare roll handy just in case.

Borders are particularly useful for providing a horizontal join between two different surfaces, so you can have a tough surface on the lower half of the wall, and something more decorative above it.

Borders are usually sold in 10 m (10 yd) lengths, so if you intend to use one measure up and calculate how many rolls you need. But bear in mind when you make your calculations that you should only join borders at the corners of the room, so you may need to buy a bit extra to allow for this.

Wallpaper Calculator

If in doubt buy an extra roll. Check that all rolls carry the same batch number, otherwise colours may vary.

Number of standard English rolls needed — American and non-standard rolls will differ.														
Height of wall from skirting	Measurement around room in metres, including doors and windows													
	10	11	12	13	14	15	16	17	18	19	20	21	22	23
2–2·2m	5	5	5	6	6	7	7	7	8	8	9	9	10	10
2·2–2·4m	5	5	6	6	7	7	8	8	9	9	10	10	10	11
2·4–2·6m	5	6	6	7	7	8	8	9	9	10	10	11	12	12
2·6–2·8m	6	6	7	7	8	8	9	9	10	11	11	12	12	12
2·8–3m	6	7	7	8	8	9	9	10	11	11	12	12	13	13
3–3·2m	6	7	8	8	9	10	10	11	11	12	12	13	13	13
3·2–3·4m	7	7	8	9	9	10	11	11	12	13	13	13	14	14

Borders can either be used on a plain painted wall, or can be stuck on to co-ordinating wallpaper to bring extra interest. This one has been used part-way up the wall, at dado height, with its companion wallpaper. But wallpaper borders can be used in all sorts of other ways as well. Apart from being hung at different heights on the wall, borders can also be used round windows and doors, as a border round the image in a picture frame or even on furniture, as shown here. This border has been used to trim the top drawer of a chest of drawers. Make sure the border is well stuck on, using suitable adhesive. If the wallcovering lacks a protective finish you can varnish over it to make it more durable, but bear in mind that this will tend to yellow it slightly.

HOW TO WALLPAPER A ROOM

Equipment

Wallpapering needs more equipment than painting, although you may have some of it already. Paperhangers' shears with 30 cm (12 in) blades are recommended for cutting and trimming wallcoverings (try to get a rust-proof pair if you can as the water in the paste can make ordinary scissors turn rusty), and a trimming knife is also useful. You will need a smoothing brush to help press the wallcovering into place and a synthetic sponge to wipe paste off the surface of the paper. A seam roller is a handy, but not essential, piece of equipment for making sure that joins are well stuck down. Do not use it on embossed paper or you will squash the pattern. You will also need a steel tape, plumb line, pencil and step ladder.

Ready-pasted wallcoverings need no pasting equipment. For other types you will need a pasting table (inexpensive folding ones are available in most hardware stores), a large

Marking the vertical is important for positioning the first drop accurately.

paintbrush or special pasting brush for pasting the paper, plus a medium-sized bucket to hold the paste. Always use the adhesive recommended by the wallcovering manufacturer. If the manufacturer does not suggest which one should be used, ask in the store. Remember that vinyls and washables, which you are most likely to be using, must be hung with a fungicidal paste to prevent mould growth as these papers take longer to dry out than uncoated ones.

Follow the instructions on page 17 above for preparing the walls prior to papering.

Hanging wallpaper

1 **Starting point** Unless the paper has a large design, start papering next to the biggest window, and work round the room from there. However, with a large pattern, centre it on the chimney breast, if there is one, between two windows or on some other focal point. Having

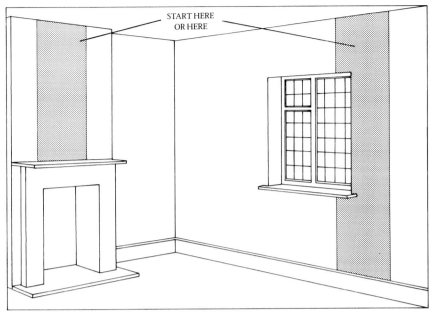

START HERE
OR HERE

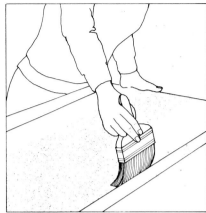

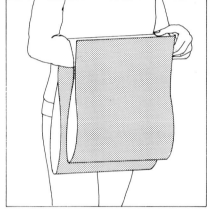

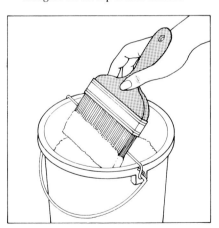

established where to start, you will need a plumb line and a pencil in order to mark a vertical line against which to place the edge of the first piece of paper.

2 **Mixing the paste** Thoroughly mix the paste in a plastic bucket, following the manufacturers' instructions on the packet. Make sure the paste is smooth and free of lumps before using. Tie a string across the top of the bucket to

scrape the excess paste off the pasting brush. You can also lay the brush across the string and the rim of the bucket to keep the handle clean while you are hanging the paper.

Centre the first drop on the chimney breast, or on some other focal point.

3 **Pasting the paper** Cut the first length of paper, allowing an extra 20 cm (8 in) for trimming. Place face down on the table with one end hanging over the end of the table and with the paper very slightly overlapping the edge of the table furthest from you. Start pasting in the centre and work outwards to the far edge. Then shift the paper to the near edge of the table, and paste towards you. When the top part of the length is done, fold it over on itself, with the paste

inside, then pull the paper along the table. Paste the lower part of the length in the same way, and fold that over as well. Leave it to soak for the amount of time specified in the paste and wallpaper manufacturers' instructions, then drape it over your arm and carry it to the wall.

4 **Hanging the paper** Unfold the top part of the length, and place it so that it exactly located against the vertical line, with about 10 cm (4 in) extra at the top for subsequent trimming. When you are sure the paper is aligned properly, start pressing it to the wall with the paper-hanging brush (for vinyl wall-covering use a sponge for smoothing down). Use long strokes and work outwards from the centre, making sure there are no air pockets. Unfold the bottom part of the length and brush on to the wall in the same way — if you measured correctly

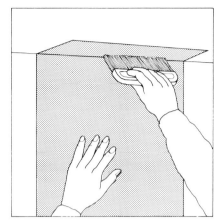

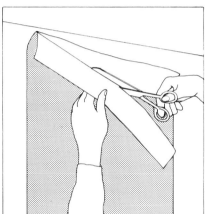

then there should be 10 cm (4 in) of spare paper at the bottom. Use the brush to dab the paper well into the angles where it meets the ceiling and the skirting board, and then crease the paper at these places with the back of a scissors' blade. Pull the paper away and trim it along the creases, then brush it back into place. Wipe off any paste which has got on to the ceiling or skirting board. Prepare the second length of paper as before, then hold it up so that it butts directly up to the first length. Slide it up or down until the pattern matches, and then brush it on to the wall, and trim the ends. Hold a piece of plain paper over the upper part of the seam, then run down the seam with a seam roller, pressing on to the seam through the plain paper — this keeps the roller off the surface of the wallpaper. Carry on in this way down to skirting level.

5 Corner When you reach a corner, measure the distance between the edge of the last length and the corner. Do this at several heights. Add 12 mm (½ in) to these measurements and 2.5 cm (1 in) for external corners, mark them on the back of the next length of paper, and draw a straight line through the marks.

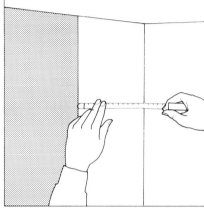

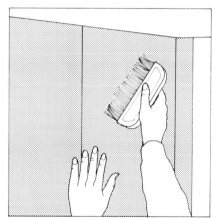

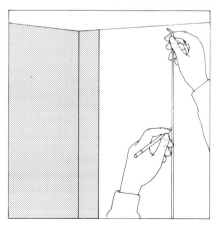

Apply paste to the paper, and then cut along the line. Hang the length with one side butting up to the previous piece, and work the paper well into the corner with the brush — the paper should overlap slightly on to the next wall. Measure the width of the remaining piece of wallpaper, add a small amount for overlap, and make a mark at the top of the wall at this distance from the corner. Using a plumb line, make a vertical line down from the mark. Apply paste to the other part of the cut length of paper, and align it to the vertical line. Brush down as usual, with the second piece of paper overlapping the first slightly in the corner. Finish off with the seam roller. If you are dealing with an external corner, then brush the first piece round the corner, making sure the overlap is stuck down well. Make a vertical line so that the second piece of paper will reach to

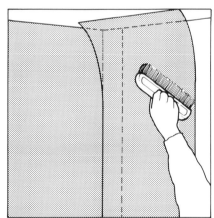

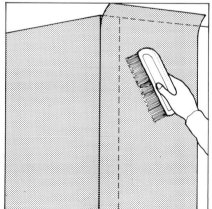

about 12 mm (½ in) from the corner, and brush down, making sure that the edge is securely fixed. Again, finish off with the seam roller. Vinyl will not stick to itself, so when using this material you will need a sharp knife to cut a straight line vertically down through both pieces in the middle of the area where they overlap. Pull away the excess pieces, and rub down with a sponge to make a butt joint.

6 **Doors** Hang the paper so that it butts to the previous length, and brush it to the wall down one side, allowing the other side to loosely hang over the door opening. Crease it into the corner from the bottom to the top of the door frame, and then cut along the crease. You will probably have enough width of wallpaper left to go some of the way across the top of the door, so crease this into the top of the frame, trim, and then

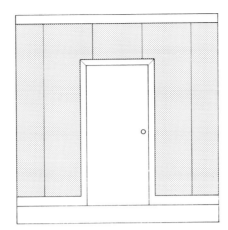

brush the whole length down well. Hang a small piece over the opening, then hang another length of paper in the same way as the first on the other side of the door.

7 **Windows** If you are papering round window frames, then use the same method as for a door. If the window has a reveal, then hang a length of wallpaper with one side butted to the preceding length, and with the other side over the opening. Make horizontal cuts along the top and bottom edge of the window reveal, fold the pieces into the reveal, crease into the corners where the reveal meets the frame, trim, and brush down. Hang short pieces above and below the window, so that they also fold into the reveal, and then hang a full length on the other side of the window, in the same way as the first. Uncovered corner

sections of the reveal can be dealt with as follows — cut a piece of paper slightly longer than the gap, brush it into the reveal, lift the previously applied piece of paper, brush the filler peice round the angle of the wall, and then brush the original piece back down again.

8 **Switches and Sockets** As always when working with electrical fittings, **switch off at the mains** before doing anything. With the wallpaper in place make diagonal cuts with scissors from the centre of the faceplate to the corners. Trim the paper to about 12 mm (½ in) from the faceplace. Loosen the screws holding the faceplate, tuck the paper behind it, and tighten the screws back down. Wall lights can be dealt with in a similar manner. Allow time for the paste to dry before switching the mains on again.

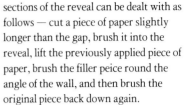

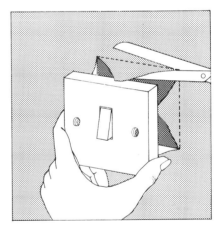

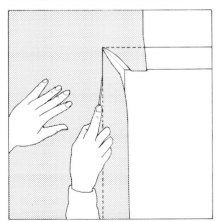

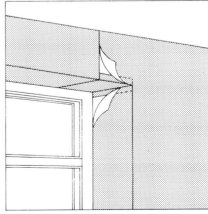

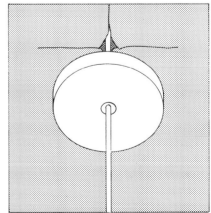

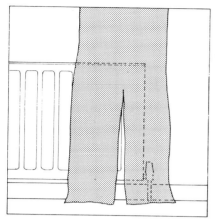

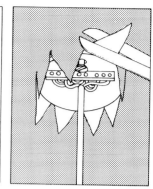

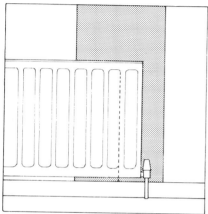

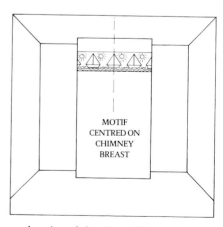

holds the folded paper up near the ceiling with a broom, the other one (not the pregnant one!) climbs on to the scaffold board and brushes the paper into place alongside the guideline. Work across the ceiling, and on reaching the wall, crease into the angle, and trim. Subsequent lengths are butted against each other, and the last piece will need to be trimmed along its length to fit. When

you encounter a ceiling rose, cut some triangular flaps until you can pass the light fitting through the hole, and dab the paper firmly against the ceiling around the rose. When the paste is dry, trim the triangular flaps with a sharp knife. Again, to be safe, **switch off at the mains** before working with electrical fittings, and do not switch on again until the paste has dried.

HANGING WALLPAPER BORDER

9 **Radiators** First turn the radiator off, and let it cool. Make marks on the top of the radiator coinciding with the position of the brackets, and measure the distance of these from the preceding edge. Mark these on the wallpaper up to the height of the top of the brackets, apply paste, and cut slit along the two lines. Hang the paper as usual, and push the strips down behind the radiator. The strips can be pressed to the wall with a radiator roller, but if you don't have one you could use a wire coat hanger wrapped in cloth.

10 **Ceilings** It is easier, and preferable, to paper ceilings when there are two people available to do the job. Arrange a scaffold board, supported on two stepladders, underneath the area where you are going to start. Mark a guideline on the ceiling for the first length, and apply paste to the paper, folding it concertina fashion. While one person

You will need

Wallpaper border (see page 37 for quantities)
Appropriate paste (see step 2 below)
Wallpapering shears

1 Decide where you want the border to go, and hold a piece against the wall to make sure it looks right in that position. If you are hanging the border next to the ceiling or cornice, it is advisable to measure down the depth of the border plus 2.5 cm (1 in), make chalk marks (check in an inconspicuous place that they will rub or wipe off) every so often and join the marks up with a metre (yard) rule. Use this as the guide-line for the lower edge of the border. The 2.5 cm (1 in) is to allow for walls and ceilings not quite being true. If you are hanging the border at dado height (i.e. at about adult's waist height) and

MOTIF
CENTRED ON
CHIMNEY
BREAST

there is no dado rail to guide you, you will need to make chalk marks on the wall about every 60 cm (2 ft), measuring up from the floor, and joining the marks with a metre (yard) rule. Likewise, if you are putting borders around windows and doors, measure carefully from the sides of

the windows and doors and construct guide-lines.

2 Cut the border to the right length (remember, there should be no joins except at the corners of the room). If it has a large design, you will need to centre the design on each wall, and in particular on a chimney breast. Then paste the border (unless it is prepasted, in which case dip it in water, following manufacturer's instructions). Make sure you are using the right type of paste. If you are sticking a vinyl border on to a vinyl wallcovering you will need special adhesive. Pat the border into position, using a soft clean cloth, at about 60 cm (2 ft) intervals. If the border is going round doors or windows it will need to be mitred. You will need a protractor for this, available very cheaply

from stationery departments if you do not already have one. If you are putting it on top of wallpaper make sure the underlying paper has completely dried out. If you are

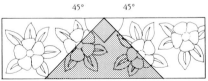

CUT OUT SHADED PIECE

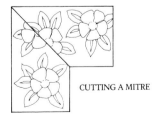

CUTTING A MITRE

Even rooms with sloping ceilings can have borders, as this picture shows. All you have to do is make sure the border is level with the ceiling and butt the lengths of border at corners or wherever there is a change of directions.

pasting the border over a textured wallcovering, before you hang the border mark the position of the border, dampen it and roll it flat with a seam roller first.

3 Step back and make sure the border looks level, then press in place properly all along its length, using the cloth and/or a seam roller.

4 Cut and paste the piece of border for the next wall, making sure it butts up to the first.

5 Continue around the room in this way.

3

FLOORING

In any room, the floor is one of the largest areas, so what you do with it is going to have a large impact on the overall room scheme. It is obviously important that you choose the flooring with the rest of the decoration strongly in mind. As no room is perfect, you may find certain visual tricks useful in correcting the look of a room. For example, since children's rooms are often small, finely patterned or plain flooring in a fairly light colour is a good choice because it gives a brighter, more spacious look to the room. Diagonal stripes on the floor also help to make a room appear bigger and, in a narrow room, stripes, running parallel to the short walls, will help make the room appear wider. However, if the room is large then intricately patterned flooring will break up the area and make it appear cosier. If the room is an irregular shape, avoid chequer-board tiles or designs with straight lines as these will only enhance the irregularities.

Children spend a large amount of time on the floor, so the flooring in a child's room must be comfortable. But the floor will also get spills on it of various kinds, so what you choose to cover it with should also be easy to clean and maintain. If you opt for an easy-clean flooring, then a light colour should not pose problems. The cleanliness aspect is also important because tiny children crawl around on their hands and knees and then put fingers into their mouths. The floor is also an important play area, so it needs to be a suitable surface for running wheeled toys along and playing with jigsaws, bricks and farm animals. The flooring must also be quiet

to walk on as you will need to creep in during the night to check up on your child. So, to sum up, suitable flooring needs to look good and be comfortable, easy to clean and quiet underfoot.

It is worth spending some time to select the flooring for a child's room because a well-chosen, good quality product is an investment and may even see your child through from babyhood to adult life. So, unless you are planning to move fairly soon or you do not mind the upheaval and expense of changing the flooring in a few years, choose something durable that neither you

nor your child will tire of and which is likely to accommodate several future changes of room schemes.

Remember, too, that all types of flooring need a smooth, level subfloor (that is, the surface on which the chosen flooring is to rest), although some floorings are slightly more tolerant of the degree of smoothness than others. Do take seriously manufacturer's recommendations in this area as the condition of the subfloor is a major factor in the durability of flooring, and the flooring in a child's room is likely to take quite a bashing anyway.

TYPES OF FLOORING AVAILABLE

Taking all these factors into account, the best type of flooring for a child's room is smooth (with the addition of non-slip rugs if you like), and the three types of flooring most worth considering are cork, vinyl and lino. Cork tiles are easy to lay (on a smooth-screeded or hardboarded subfloor) and are warm, quiet and resilient to walk on. The best type has a non-porous clear vinyl wear surface and a vinyl backing. If laid properly, these PVC-coated tiles are very easy to keep clean and very durable — they can last for up to about twenty years. Although they are not initially cheap, they represent an investment if you are not planning on moving in the foreseeable future.

PVC-coated cork tiles are also available

with attractive wood veneers under the wear layer. These come in 'plank' or tile forms which, when laid, look very much like a hardwood floor but with the resilience and ease of laying of cork.

However, cork cannot be used with some types of underfloor heating and it tends to come in a limited range of natural colours. These natural colours are very attractive nevertheless, and will harmonize with many colour schemes.

Cushioned vinyl is another good choice because, like cork, it is warm, easy to clean, resilient and easy to lay, although if you have any doubts about your ability ask the store to recommend a qualified fitter, as the better laid this type of flooring is, the longer it will last. Cushioned vinyl comes in sheet form in various widths (to minimize wastage and joins) and in a wide variety of colours and patterns — some look very convincingly like other types of floor coverings such as parquet. This type of flooring is usually available in a range of qualities and it is always advisable, if you can afford it, to buy the best quality you can afford. Do not buy cushioned vinyl that is less than 1.4 mm ($^1/_{16}$ in) thick, and look for ranges that have glass fibre 'stay-flat' layers sandwiched in the vinyl to prevent the flooring curling up or shrinking. The better the quality of the lino, usually the thicker the transparent PVC 'wear-layer'. This is the actual surface that you walk on and it is this that protects the design underneath from wear and scuffs.

Ordinary vinyl is not as warm and resilient as the cushioned type, but it is still worth considering. Vinyl tiles are colourful and easier to lay than sheet vinyl, but are not as tolerant of slight unevennesses in the subfloor. Most types of vinyl (cushioned and uncushioned) can be used with underfloor heating, although this is not the case with all types, so if you have underfloor heating and you are opting for vinyl, check that the sort you buy is suitable, and don't exceed the recommended maximum thermostat temperature for the product.

Lino is an old favourite that is coming back with a new image. Although not as resilient as cushioned vinyl, it is an extremely hardwearing product and during the first ten years after it is laid it actually gets tougher. It is suitable for use with underfloor heating up to 27°C (80°F). Lino is also very easy to maintain and, as the colour goes right through the product, scuffs and scratches hardly show. As all the ingredients are natural, lino is a 'green' product and this combination of ingredients creates a natural bactericidal action and makes lino very resistant to most stains, so it is perfect for small children's rooms. Lino comes in a range of lovely subtle colours in soft tones, and can be intercut to form intricate patterns. Lino does, however, need a very smooth subfloor and also needs professional laying as it is very stiff.

Carpeting

You may, however, feel that you want to put carpet down in your child's room because it feels warm and cosy, offers sound insulation and is softer to fall on. But as children often like to play with toy cars and other wheeled toys on their bedroom floor they may find carpet a rather frustrating obstacle to their games, so remember this when weighing up which would be the best flooring for a child's room. Carpet is also, of course, not as hygienic or easy to keep clean as smooth floorings. The types of carpets that are easiest to keep clean are the new generation stain-resistant nylon carpets. Many of them are good quality, look very similar to wool and are hard-wearing. Do not, however, expect miracles from the 'stain-resist' aspect. These carpets are not stain-*proof* only stain resistant. That means stains still need to be dealt with carefully and quickly, and some substances will stain whatever you do. Strongly coloured and patterned carpet helps hide soiling and staining, but remember these types of designs are best saved for larger rooms otherwise they will look too overpowering.

Normal 'bedroom' carpets are not designed to take heavy wear, so when buying a carpet for a child's room choose a heavy-duty one, with a really tight, dense pile for longer life. Do not try to economize unless you really have to, or you will end up with something that will look shabby in no time. To compare pile densities in the showroom, bend samples back on themselves, pile side outwards. The less of the backing you can see at the base of the pile, the denser the weave. Unless you choose foam-backed carpet, be sure to allow for good quality underlay in your budget as this makes all the difference to the comfort and life of the carpet.

Cord carpets and carpet tiles are also very hard-wearing, though not as soft and resilient as normal pile carpet. Carpet tiles have the added advantage that stained areas can be lifted up and put under the tap, or discarded and replaced and, unlike ordinary carpet, you can quite easily lay them yourself and they require no underlay.

RUGS

As mentioned before, a good combination for a child's room floor is smooth flooring with perhaps one or more rugs if you feel it needs a touch of extra cosiness. Rugs are very useful because they can be placed just where you want them, they bring extra pattern and colour to the floor, they can be rolled up and taken with you if you move house and they can also be rolled up and taken to the cleaners, if necessary.

It is important that rugs lying on smooth floors have non-slip backings (available separately as rubberized mesh — cut slightly smaller than the rug and placed underneath) and that the rug is substantial enough to lie flat so that small feet do not get caught underneath it. If you place a rug on top of a carpet it may still ruckle up, in which case you will need special non-slip rug-backing for use with carpets. A word of caution if you do put a rug on top of a carpet — if the rug has strong colours it may not be colour-fast and colour can be transferred to the carpet below if anything is spilt on the rug.

Rugs can be bought ready-made, made up from kits or you can make them yourself from scratch. Most objects in children's rooms are likely to receive spills and be the victim of accidents at one time or another, so if you buy a ready-made rug do not get one that is precious, or that you will worry about too much. Avoid rugs that cannot be cleaned, or else just buy very cheap ones and plan to chuck them out in a few years. There are rugs available with special children's designs on them, but you do not have to opt for one of these. Consider dhurries (flat-woven cotton rugs from India), which come in lovely designs and colours, and fluffy white flokatis from Greece.

Kits are available for tufted and needlepoint rugs, and if you would like to have a go at making your own rug but do not feel ready to create your own design, then these kits will give confidence. However, designing and making your own rugs is fun, and will give you an even greater sense of satisfaction when you have completed one yourself.

Making a hand-tufted rug
You will need

Rug canvas with 10 holes to 7.5 cm (3 in) —
buy a piece 8 cm (3½ in) bigger all round
than the finished design

Masking tape

A latch hook

Ready-cut rug yarn in colours to match your
design

A large blunt needle

Carpet thread

1 Decide how big you want the finished rug
to be, then work out your design on graph
paper in proportion, bearing in mind that
there will be 10 squares to every 7.5 cm
(3 in), and that each square will equal one
knot.

2 You can either work from the chart, or
draw the design on to the canvas with a
marker pen, leaving a 8 cm (3½ in) border
all round the edge of the canvas. Bind the
edge of the canvas with masking tape to
prevent it fraying.

*Cushioned vinyl is particularly
suitable for children's rooms as it is
warm, comfortable and easy to keep
clean, as well as available in a range
of very attractive colours and designs.
Thanks to a layer of bubbles
sandwiched in the middle of the
product, cushioned vinyl makes a
very comfortable surface on which to
crawl and play. Easy for anyone
competent at diy to lay, this type of
flooring offers very good value and,
properly laid, should give years of
good service. For best results lay this
type of flooring on a smooth subfloor.*

This beautifully co-ordinated room scheme is given a finishing touch with this matching tufted rug. This rug is sold ready-made, but tufted rugs are also available from some manufacturers in kit form or you can make a rug from scratch yourself, designing your own pattern and choosing your own colours. Hand tufting a rug is time-consuming, but once you have finished you will feel a real sense of achievement!

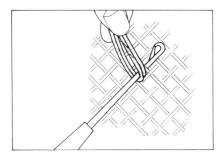

3 Start tufting in one corner of the rug: take two lengths of yarn together, fold them in half, loop them around the hook below the latch.

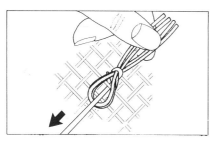

4 Take the rug hook and close the latch. Hold the ends of the wool in one hand, and push the hook into the canvas and up through a hole in the same row with the other. Open the latch with your fingers and put the ends of yarn under the hook.

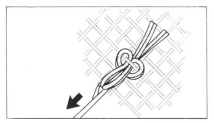

5 Pull the hook back through the canvas. The latch will close and bring the ends of the yarn with it to form a knot.

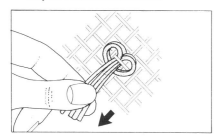

6 Pull the knot tight by hand.

7 Continue working across the rug in rows.

8 When you have finished, fold the 8 cm (3½ in) border to the back of the rug and sew it in place using the large needle and carpet thread.

Making a quilted patchwork rug

You can mix printed and plain cotton fabrics in this soft and squashy rug, but make sure the fabrics are of a similar weight. For a small baby it makes a lovely play mat, for the older child a welcoming bedside rug.

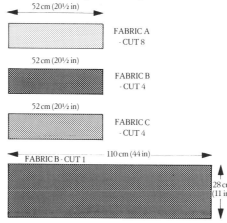

You will need

Fabric A — eight pieces measuring 52 × 14.5 cm (20½ × 5½ in).
Fabric B — four pieces 52 cm × 14.5 cm (20½ × 5½ in), plus one strip 110 cm × 28 cm (44 × 11 in).
Fabric C — four pieces 52 × 14.5 cm (20½ × 5½ in).

Piece of cotton fabric for the back, 102 cm (40½ in) square
Piece of medium to thick polyester wadding, 102 cm (40½ in) square

1 Cut out the strips of fabric.

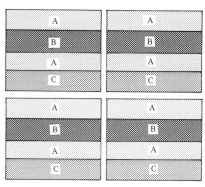

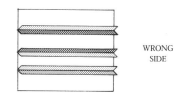

2 Take the pieces measuring 52 × 14.5 cm (20½ × 5½ in) and lay them out next to each other, right side up, to form four squares, each square starting with a strip of fabric A, then a strip of fabric B, then a strip of fabric A, then a strip of fabric C. Sew the strips in each square together, right sides facing, taking a 1 cm (½ in) seam allowance, to form four squares.

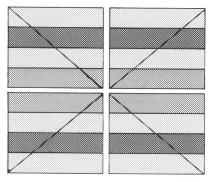

3 Lay the squares out to form a large square, with fabric A at the top of the

two squares and at the bottom of the two bottom squares. Draw a line (using pencil, tailor's chalk or vanishing marker) diagonally from the top left hand corner to the bottom right hand corner of the top left and bottom right squares. Draw a diagnonal line from the top right hand corner to the bottom left hand corner of the top right and bottom left hand squares. Cut along these lines.

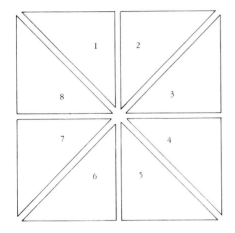

4 Swop triangles 3 and 4 with each other and swivel them round so that the triangles of fabric A now lie in the centre. Repeat with triangles 7 and 8.

5 Sew all the sections together, right sides together, taking 1 cm (½ in) seams. Start by sewing sections 1 and 7 together, 2 and 4 together, 3 and 5 together and 6 and 8 together. Then sew the top two squares together and the bottom two

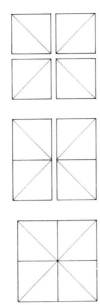

squares together. Finally, join the centre seam. Press all seams open as you work.

6 Lay the backing fabric out wrong side up, lay the wadding on top and then lay the patchwork, right side upward on top. Tack the three layers together in lines all over, using big stitches.

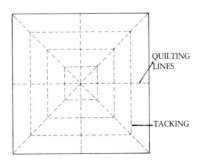

7 Machine or hand quilt (using small running stitches) along all seam lines, sewing through all thicknesses.

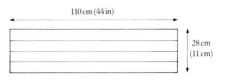

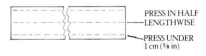

8 Cut the strip of fabric B measuring 110 × 28 cm (44 × 11 in) into four long strips 110 × 7 cm (44 × 2½ in). Press them in half longways, then press under 1 cm (½ in) along each raw edge.

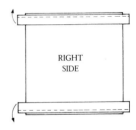

9 Take two strips, open them out and lay them along opposite edges of the quilt, right sides together and raw edges level. Have equal excess fabric at either end. Machine along the 1 cm (½ in) fold line.

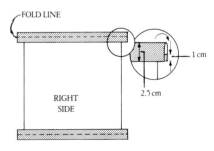

10 Fold the strip over the raw edges, fold under 1 cm (½ in) along the raw edges of the strip and slip stitch in place on the back of the fabric.

This plump and inviting quilted rug can be used initially as a baby play mat and later as a comfy bedside rug. It it not difficult to make yourself and is washable too. The patchwork duvet cover can be made in matching fabric to form a set.

11 Take the other two strips, open them out and lay them along the remaining two edges of the quilt, right sides together and raw edges level. Have equal excess fabric at either end. Machine along the 1 cm (½ in) fold line, across the corners of the first two strips. Trim the ends of the first two strips.

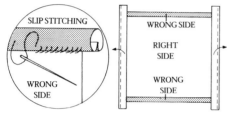

12 Trim the excess fabric at either end to 1 cm (½ in) and press these 1 cm (½ in) pieces to the wrong side.

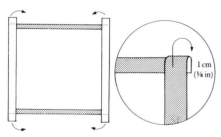

13 Fold the strip over the raw edges, fold under 1 cm (½ in) along the raw edges of the strips and slip stitch in place on the back of the quilt, oversewing the corners.

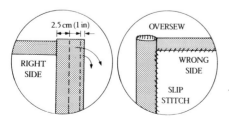

This floor consists simply of chipboard squares which have been stained to form a road layout and then coated with polyurethane varnish. Although not a particularly attractive surface, chipboard is perfect for playing on with toy cars and the addition of the painted lines turns it into something really special and of great potential.

As chipboard is laid as an alternative to floorboards and is not very common as a flooring material, if you wish to copy this idea the best way is to use uncoated cork tiles. Although they are not as durable as the PVC-coated type, they are very much less expensive and are easy to put colour on to.

Lay the tiles but do not varnish them. Then draw a plan on squared paper, showing the available floor space in the room (i.e. not covered by furniture) and the arrangement of the tiles. On this you can plan out the arrangement of the roadways. Copy

your plan on the tiles using a ruler, compass and straight-edge — or draw freehand if you prefer the idea of winding lanes! Paint in the roads using two or three coats of coloured varnish (mix-to-order paint ranges do the best range of colours). When these are dry, cover the whole floor with several coats of polyurethane varnish, following the manufacturer's instructions.

4

WINDOWS

The windows in a nursery need some sort of covering. As with any other room this is necessary for privacy, to keep light out when the occupant is asleep and to keep warmth in during the winter (this last point is less important if you have double glazing). Window coverings can bring an extra splash of colour and pattern into the room and are also useful for masking an unattractive view, for example, should the room look on to a brick wall.

Unless you particularly want a really frilly, extravagant look for your child's room, your best option is to keep the window treatment fairly simple. If you opt for curtains, they should be sill-length. Floor-length curtains could be tugged down by a boisterous toddler, and at the very least will probably get dirty finger marks on them. Tie-backs and valances are not essential and will not be noticed by a baby anyway.

Opt for a washable cotton fabric, preferably in a wide width, so you will not have to have seams running down the middle of the curtains. Ask if the fabric is likely to shrink and if so, by how much. You can choose a strongly patterned fabric to fit in with the room scheme, an abstract or geometric design to co-ordinate with other colours or patterns in the room, or a plain colour which can either tone in with the scheme or contrast with it. Also check that the fabric drapes nicely and will fall into pleats easily.

Remember that a strongly patterned fabric, particularly if it is specifically a 'children's' design, will probably have a shorter life than something plainer because the child (and maybe you!) will tire of it sooner. Big designs are also less economical on fabric than smaller ones because you will need a certain amount extra to match up the repeat. On curtains that require several drops this can amount to quite a lot of wasted fabric. However, you may be able to use the off-cuts for patchwork and appliqué, or for making accessories such as cushion covers and storage bags.

On the other hand, curtains can be a good place for introducing large expanses of pattern, and changing curtains is less difficult than, for example, changing wallpaper. You may see a fabric that you find so charming you just have to buy it, even though you know it will probably need replacing in a couple of years time.

It also makes sense to choose the simplest type of curtain heading. Curtains need some sort of fullness in them even when they are drawn, otherwise they look very mean. The way that curtains get this fullness is by sewing the top edge of the fabric on to curtain tape and gathering it up with the draw-cords in the tape. There are different tapes available, which give different configurations of gathers. These configurations are known as 'curtain headings' and some are very elaborate and use a lot of fabric. The results look very tailored, generous and full, but are rather out of place in a nursery. Also, if you choose a fabric with an interesting pattern and you have the curtains too gathered, the design will end up hidden in the folds and the impact will be lost.

LININGS

Curtains, ideally, should be lined. The one advantage of unlined curtains is that they are easier to wash (assuming the fabric is washable in the first place). However, unlined curtains let in a lot of light and they do not insulate very well, so they are less suitable for a nursery, unless you team them with a blind.

Curtain lining also helps protect the fabric from fading, dust, dirt and condensation. It helps curtains look and feel more substantial and hang better, and the effect looks neater from the outside, too. Curtain linings are either sewn in permanently, or they can be detachable, which means that they hook on to the back of the curtain fabric and can be removed for washing. This is particularly useful if a dry-clean-only lining has been teamed with a washable curtain fabric, for example, or if the curtain fabric gets dirtier more quickly than the lining.

There are several different types of curtain lining fabrics, each of which do a different job. Whichever you choose, try to buy the best quality as it can make all the difference to the apperance of the curtains. Ordinary curtain lining is made from cotton sateen, which is strong, drapes well and has a shiny surface which resists dust. It is available in a wide range of colours to co-ordinate with virtually all curtain fabrics. There are also thermal linings which are specially treated to keep the warmth in during the winter and the heat out during the summer. The best-known of this type of lining is 'Milium'.

Rather than buying fabric that is specifically for lining curtains, you may prefer to back the curtains with a co-ordinating fabric. This makes a real feature of the lining and looks extra special if you bind the edges of the curtains in a contrast or co-ordinating colour (see the picture on page 7). It is important, however, to choose a pattern and a colourway that is not so strong as to show through on the front fabric. Remember that light, maybe even strong sunlight, will be shining through the fabrics, so check the effect before you go ahead with this idea.

CURTAIN TRACKS AND POLES

Curtains usually hang from tracks or poles and, as there are considerable variations in design, it is important to choose the right type for your needs. Some, for example, are stronger than others. Poles vary in thickness and metal tracks tend to be stronger than plastic ones. It is unlikely that you are going to hang heavy curtains in a nursery, but if you are then it is important to buy a suitably strong track or pole. It is also important that it is firmly fixed to the wall and well supported along its length.

Tracks or poles should also be wide enough to allow the fabric to be drawn well back from the window on either side, otherwise the curtains will obscure some of the light. So when you measure up for a track of pole, take this into account, and remember that the wider the window and the bulkier the curtains, the more spare track you will need on either side. If there is not enough room (in the case of a dormer window, for example) to extend the track to either side of the window, consider using a blind instead (see below).

The most suitable poles for a child's room are wooden ones in a light colour. Plain, unfinished poles and rings are also available which you can paint or varnish yourself to fit in with the room scheme. Painting the rings and different parts of the poles in several colours picked out from the curtain fabric can create a stunning effect.

If you opt for curtain track, then choose one that is as discreet as possible. With some designs, the track is completely hidden by the curtains when they are drawn. Others have a very plain track, below which the curtains hang. Sometimes it is possible to paint or stick wallpaper on to the surface of track to camouflage it. For bay and curved windows choose a curtain track that is designed to bend or have one made to measure.

NET CURTAINS

For additional privacy, for example if the nursery is overlooked, you may feel the need for some sort of net curtaining. Net curtains can look rather drab, particularly if they are hung on stretch wires. It does not take much extra effort to come up with something that looks more attractive, both inside and outside your home. Using proper net curtain track and transparent net curtain heading tape makes the curtains look more special. As net is a very light-weight fabric you will need about 2½ to 3 times the finished width of the window to create a full enough effect. Bear in mind that net curtain is usually sold by depth not width, generally with ready-made hems top and bottom. This means that you should buy the length of fabric you want for the width of the curtains you need.

As net can look a bit dull, you can also add a border of the main curtain fabric at the bottom and/or sides to give more body and a more stylish look. In a more traditional home you could use cotton lace. This has the benefit of being a more natural colour than the bluey-whiteness of Terylene (although sheer curtains can be any colour you like — you can dye Terylene easily at home). For a simpler effect you can use fine cotton lawn, voile or muslin. Another alternative is to use translucent blinds (see below).

BLINDS

Although curtains tend to be the automatic choice for window coverings, you should also consider blinds for a nursery. Blinds have the advantages of pulling up out of the way when not in use, taking up less room where space is limited (for example, with a dormer window), and of bringing strong colour or bold, flat pattern into the room scheme. Alternatively, curtains can be used in conjunction with blinds to create a very flexible window treatment.

Venetian blinds have metal or wooden slats

which can be tilted to alter the amount of light that comes in, or lifted right up out of the way. They are usually custom-made to fit the exact window size, although some are available ready-made in standard sizes and can be cut down by the purchaser, if necessary, for an exact fit.

Venetian blinds are very durable as a window covering and will last for years provided the slats are not bent or the mechanism damaged by rough treatment. The metal variety in particular are available in a very wide range of colours and finishes. Some have special thermal finishes on the back of the slats, some have patterns printed on them, some have metallic finishes and some are finely perforated and act like high-tech net curtains. With this last type you do need an additional window covering because at night, when the lights are on, people outside can see into the room. One

disadvantage of venetian blinds is that they can be tricky to clean. A frequent flick over with a feather duster is probably the best solution.

A roller blind consists of a piece of flat, stiffened fabric. This is fixed to a roller which either has a spring mechanism at one end and a pull cord in the middle, or a simple pulley and continuous pull cord at one end. This is then hung on a pair of brackets. A roller blind is very economical on fabric: unlike curtains it needs no fullness. The traditional fabric is holland — a plain, stiffened fabric which does not fray along its raw edges. Or you can use cotton fabric and treat it with a special stiffening spray. As an alternative to net curtains, roller blinds can be made from lace and translucent fabrics. Some designs are also available with a rubberized backing.

Roller blinds can be bought made-to-measure. Alternatively, you can buy a ready-

made blind and cut it to fit, if necessary (this type is only available in standard sizes) or you can make a blind yourself from a kit, which is not difficult. Like venetian blinds, the roller blind mechanism can be damaged by rough treatment so it is important that children are taught to use one of these blinds properly and not play with it.

Of the other main types of fabric blinds — roman, austrian and festoon — roman are the most suitable for a nursery because they are simple in design. When they are pulled down they look rather like roller blinds, but when pulled up they form neat, horizontal pleats. Roman blinds are available made-to-measure, in kit form and you can also make them yourself from scratch fairly easily. Like roller blinds, roman blinds are very economical on fabric, though they are a little more complicated to make, as they have a system of dowels and cords at the back.

MAKING CURTAINS

Measuring up

If you are using the standard curtain tape suggested here, you will need 1½-2 times the width of the pole or track (not the width of the window). Double the width looks best, particularly if the fabric is fairly light-weight. If the fabric is heavy, you can get away with less. Err on the side of generosity when buying curtain fabric. If you are on a tight budget, opt for larger quantities of something cheaper rather than skimp on something pricey.

To calculate the number of lengths of fabric you need, multiply the width of the track by the fullness (i.e. 1½ or 2) then divide by the width of the fabric. Round up to the nearest whole number. This is the number of lengths of fabric you will need.

To calculate the total amount of fabric needed, measure from the hook suspension point on the track or pole (i.e. the small rings that the hooks go into) to the sill. To this measurement add 20 cm (8 in) for hems, heading and shrinkage. Multiply this

measurement by the number of lengths required to calculate the total amount of fabric needed.

Take the pattern repeat into account when estimating the amount of fabric you need to make curtains, since the motifs on all drops should line up. If the fabric has a large repeat you will need extra fabric. Find out the depth of the repeat and multiply it by the number of fabric lengths you are using. Add this number to the total amount of fabric needed. This tells you how much extra fabric you need. If the fabric has a particularly big design, it is better to have a whole motif near the bottom of a curtain, rather than having it near the top or chopping it in half.

If you are making linings for curtains, you will need slightly less fabric than for the main curtains, as linings should be shorter than the curtains themselves and do not need a deep turning at the top edge. The exact amount depends on the lining method you have chosen so consult the relevant section below for details. If the width of your chosen lining

fabric is very different from the curtain fabric, you will need to make separate calculations for the amount of lining fabric you will need, following the process above. Detachable linings only need 1½ times the width, sewn-in linings need the same as for the curtains.

General points for making curtains

○ Work out your calculations on paper and draw a diagram to show how the lengths fit together.
○ If you have an odd number of lengths you must cut one of them in half and position it on the outer edge of each curtain.
○ Fabric needs to be laid out flat for cutting — the floor is probably the best place, so move furniture if necessary.
○ Cut the first length carefully, making sure any motifs are in the best position.
○ A large motif should be towards the bottom of the curtain, not near the top or cut in half.

Measuring up for curtains

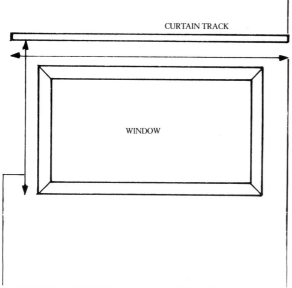

ALLOW EXTRA AT SIDES SO THAT CURTAIN CAN PULL WELL OUT OF THE WAY OF THE WINDOW

CURTAIN TRACK

WINDOW

FOR THE NUMBER OF LENGTHS, MULTIPLY THE WIDTH BY 1½ OR 2, DEPENDING ON HOW FULL YOU WANT THE CURTAINS TO BE, THEN DIVIDE BY THE WIDTH OF THE FABRIC

FOR THE CURTAIN LENGTH, MEASURE FROM THE TRACK OR POLE RINGS TO THE SILL, ALLOWING FOR HEMS, HEADING AND SHRINKAGE, THEN MULTIPLY BY THE NUMBER OF LENGTHS

3 Cut off the selvedges as these can cause puckering. If you do not wish to do this you can clip into the selvedges every 5 cm (2 in) to reduce the tension.

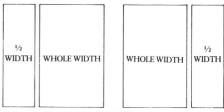

½ WIDTH | WHOLE WIDTH | WHOLE WIDTH | ½ WIDTH

3 DROPS DIVIDED INTO 2 CURTAINS

4 Lay out the lengths to produce two curtains of equal width. If you have an odd number of drops, you will have to cut one drop in half. These should be positioned on the outer edges of the two curtains, making a left- and a right-hand curtain.

5 If the curtains are made up of more than one length then these will have to be joined. Unlined curtains should be joined with 1.5 cm (⅝ in) flat fell seams, matching up any pattern exactly across the joins: this type of seam looks much

○ When cutting the lengths, make sure you cut exactly at right angles to the selvedge.

○ Use the first length as a template for all the others, matching any pattern repeats.

Making a pair of simple unlined curtains

Although unlined curtains let in more light than lined curtains, they are cheaper and quicker to make and are easier to wash. You can always add detachable linings at a later date or, alternatively, you can team unlined curtains with a blind.

You will need

Fabric calculated as above

Standard curtain tape — as long as the width of the curtain fabric plus 20 cm (8 in) for turnings

Curtain hooks — buy the right sort for the tape and the number required for the length of the tape

1 Lay out the fabric and check it for flaws before you cut it (you cannot take it back once it has been cut). Making sure that you have any pattern running in the correct direction, measure out the first length, taking into account the position of any motifs. Draw a cutting line with tailor's chalk exactly at right angles to the selvedge and cut. Write TOP on the back of the top edge with tailor's chalk.

2 Repeat for the number of drops you require. You can use the first length as a template for all the others, matching any pattern repeats so they occur in the same position on each drop. This may mean discarding a piece of fabric between each drop if you have a pattern repeat.

A small window in a nursery is given an unusual treatment by the asymmetric use of two roller blinds. Teamed with a bright and cheerful curtain fabric, the blinds keep out considerably more light than the unlined curtains would do on their own.

The curtains have been gathered using standard curtain tape and are hung on a plain and simple curtain track which blends into the paintwork and becomes almost invisible.

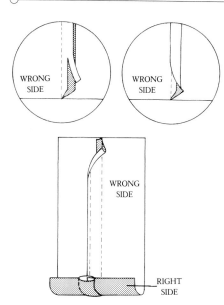

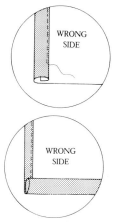

neater from outside as the raw edges are completely hidden. If, however, you are going to line the curtains with detachable linings you can use ordinary seams and press them open. To make a flat fell seam, sew an ordinary 1.5 cm (⅝ in) seam, right sides together. With the wrong side facing, cut one seam allowance in half and fold the other seam allowance over it. Press the seam allowance flat so the trimmed allowance is underneath. Tack in place then machine top stitch close to the fold.

6 Turn the outer side edges under 1 cm (⅜ in), then 1.5 cm (⅝ in) to the wrong side and machine in place.

7 Turn the bottom edge under 7.5 cm

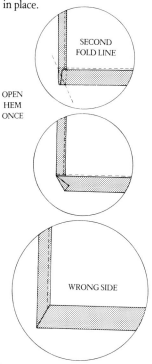

(3 in) to the wrong side, then a further 7.5 cm (3 in) to form a double hem. Press in place.

8 To mitre the corners, unfold the hem once and fold in the corner running from the last hem fold to the inner edge of the side seam. Press in place and fold the hem back again.

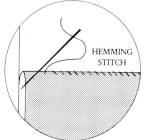

9 Hand-hem the mitre and hem in place.

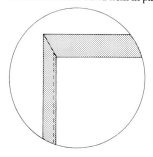

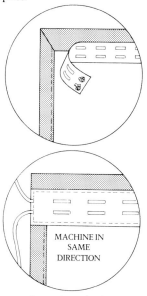

10 To position the curtain tape in place, turn under a 5 cm (2 in) single hem to the wrong side along the top edge, mitring the corners. Press, pin and tack in place.

11 Cut two pieces of standard curtain tape 10 cm (4 in) longer than the width of each finished curtain. At one end of each piece of tape, pull a 5 cm (2 in) piece of each cord through to the back and knot securely. Trim the tape to within 1.5 cm (⅝ in) of the knot and press this to the wrong side. Position these ends of the tape at the centre edges of the curtains (i.e. the edges where the curtains will meet) and pin in place, covering the raw edge of the top turning and with the top edge of the tape 2.5 cm (1 in) below the top of the curtain. At the outer edges of each curtain pull the cords through to the front of the tape, trim the tape 1.5 cm (⅝ in) beyond the curtain edge. Turn this to the wrong side. Tack the tape in place them machine along both long edges of the tape, close to the edge and avoiding the cords. Both rows of machining should be done in the same direction to avoid puckering the tape. Machine across the short ends of the tape, being careful not to trap the pull cords in the stitching, and remove tacking.

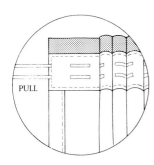

12 Draw up the cords from the outer edges of the curtain, pleating the curtains evenly until they are the right width. Tie the cords together and tuck out of sight but do not cut them off: you will need to put the curtains out flat for washing or cleaning.

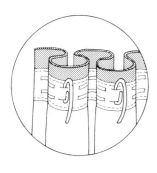

13 Insert hooks in the tape about every 8 cm (3¼ in) and hang on the pole or track, making sure you put the left and right curtains the correct way round.

Making a pair of detachable linings

Detachable linings are simple to make and can be made in conjunction with a pair of curtains, or they can be added to unlined curtains at a later date. You also only need 1½ times the width of the track, so they are economical on fabric. You can choose ordinary lining, thermal lining or black-out lining.

Measuring up

The exact amount of fabric required depends on the hanging method you choose. Either you can hang the lining on the same hooks as the curtains, or you can use special combined hooks and gliders. In both cases you will need 1½ times the track width. If you are using the same hooks as the curtain, each length of lining fabric must be 7.5 cm (3 in) longer than the length of the finished curtains; the lining needs to be 2.5 cm (1 in) shorter at the bottom, and you need 5 cm (2 in) less fabric at the top edge, making 7.5 cm (3 in) less in total, but you need to add 15 cm (6 in) for the bottom hem. If you are using combined hooks and gliders subtract an extra 2.5 cm (1 in) per length, meaning each length of lining fabric needs to be 5 cm (2 in) longer than the length of the finished curtains.

You will need

Lining fabric — for measuring up, follow the instructions above and for curtains
Lining tape — as long as the total width of the lining fabric plus 20 cm (8 in) for turnings

1 Make up the linings as for simple unlined curtains as far as stage 9. However, you do not need flat fell seams, so simply use ordinary 1.5 cm (⅝ in) seams and press them open on the wrong side.

LINING TAPE RIGHT WAY UP, RIGHT SIDE FACING RIGHT SIDE OF LINING

2 Cut two pieces of lining tape, each 10 cm (4 in) longer than the fabric widths. Lining tape is, in section, like an upside-down Y. The right side of the tape is the side where the cords are visible.

3 Pull out about 5 cm (2 in) of cord from the ends of the two pieces of tape which will be at the centre of the curtains when finished (remember you will have a left and a right hand curtain). Knot these ends together and trim the tape to the knots.

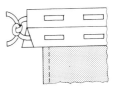

RIGHT SIDE OF LINING

4 Pin the lining tape on to the top of the linings, sandwiching the fabric between the lower flaps and having the knotted ends at the centre edges of the lining, with the tape projecting beyond the centre edges by 1 cm (⅜ in). Before you tack or sew the tape in place, insert some of the hooks into the tape and check against the curtain fabric, on the track or pole, that the lining is short enough (it should be about 2.5 cm (1 in) shorter than the curtains). If not, unpin the tape and trim enough off the top of the linings so that they will hang at the right length.

5 Tack the tape in place, making sure you catch the back flap of the tape as well. Turn the centre 1 cm (⅜ in) tape overhangs under twice to the wrong side to form a double hem, and tack in place, but leave the knots at the front. On the outer edges of the tape pull the cords free, to the front of the tape, for about 5 cm (2 in). Trim the tape to form 1 cm (⅜ in) overhangs, neaten as for the centre tape ends, and tack in place.

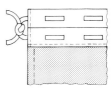

6 Machine along the bottom of the tape, close to the edge, then machine down the short ends, making sure the cords on the outer edges are still free for gathering. Remove tacking.

7 Gather up the linings evenly so they are
   the same width as the finished curtains.
   With the wrong side of the curtains and

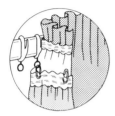

the wrong side of the lining together,
either slide the curtain hooks into the
lining tape or slot hooks into the lining
tape every 8 cm (3¼ in) and hook them
into the rings below the runners of the
curtain hooks (if your track has combined
gliders and hooks).

8 To hold the lining in place at the sides you
   can sew Velcro dots to the side hems of
   the lining and curtains, about every 30 cm
   (12 in). These dots should be sewn in by
   hand and this is best done when the
   curtains are actually hanging up, so you
   can check that they line up exactly.

Making a pair of simple curtains with a sewn-in lining

A sewn-in lining is really the best type of
lining to have as it improves the hang of
curtains and makes them look their best.
Make sure both the curtain fabric and the
lining fabric are washable.

Measuring up

For the amount of curtain fabric you will
need, see the section above on measuring up
for unlined curtains. The lining fabric should
be the same size as the curtain fabric, less

6 cm (2½ in) from each drop. The overall
width of the lining fabric for each curtain
should be 3 cm (1¼ in) less than the overall
width of the curtain fabric (e.g. if there are
two lengths of fabric making up each curtain,
each length of lining fabric should be 1.5 cm
(⅝ in) narrower than the curtain fabric).

You will need

Fabric calculated as above
Lining fabric calculated as above
Tailor's chalk
Standard curtain tape — as long as the width
   of the curtain fabric plus 20 cm (8 in) for
   turnings
Curtain hooks — buy the right sort to go
   with the tape and the number required for
   the length of the tape

1 Cut the curtain fabric and lining fabric,
   following steps 1-4 for unlined curtains.

*Soft, though not pastel, colours and
an array of patterns together create a
wonderful summery effect in this
child's room. The maypole design on
the bound-edged curtains (lined with
yellow gingham) is emphasized by the
candy-striped roman blinds.
Although there is a variety of patterns
and colourways on the cushion
covers, giving a casual look, they all
co-ordinate and the overall effect is
one of harmony.*

*The window seat, with its useful
drawers and cheerful, fishy handles
provides a lovely place for an older
child to sit and daydream. The
dragged paintwork gives a friendly
and informal finish and a thin foam
mattress and a bolster, both covered
in pink gingham, form the basic
seating arrangements. The seat is
especially useful because it can also
become instant sleeping
accommodation for a friend.*

Make any necessary joins using 1.5 cm (⅝ in) open seams and press them open.

2 At the top edge of the curtain fabric, on the wrong side, mark the centre point with tailor's chalk. Also do this on the

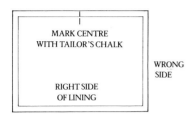

MARK CENTRE
WITH TAILOR'S CHALK

RIGHT SIDE
OF LINING

WRONG
SIDE

right side of the top edge of the lining fabric.

3 Lay the lining fabric on top of the curtain fabric, right sides together. Pin and tack the side seams together, with raw edges level (do not worry that the curtain fabric is wider than the lining) and the

WRONG SIDE
OF LINING
FABRIC

RIGHT SIDE OF
CURTAIN FABRIC

top edge of the lining 4 cm (1½ in) below the top edge of the curtain fabric. Take a 1 cm (⅜ in) seam allowance.

4 Measure down from the top of the lining (which will be the top of the finished curtain) and mark the finished length of the curtain with tailor's chalk on both seam allowances of the lining. Make another mark 7.5 cm (3 in) above the existing marks. This is the sewing line for the hem.

WRONG SIDE
OF LINING
FABRIC

RIGHT SIDE

5 Machine stitch the side seams of the curtains, taking a 1 cm (⅜ in) seam and stopping 10 cm (4 in) short of the upper mark.

6 Press the seams open, then turn the fabric right sides out. Line up the chalk marks at the top of the fabric and press

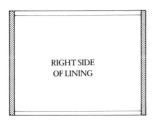

RIGHT SIDE
OF LINING

the side seams flat. There should be a 1.5 cm (⅝ in) strip of curtain fabric showing either side of the lining on the wrong side.

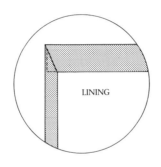

LINING

7 Still on the wrong side of the curtain, fold the top strip of fabric down over the top edge of the lining, tucking in the corners to form 'mock mitres'. Tack along the raw edge.

8 Apply the curtain tape as for unlined curtains.

9 Turn the curtain and lining inside out again. Turn up a double hem of about

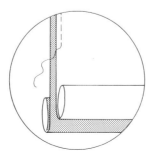

15 cm (6 in) — i.e. turn up a hem of 7.5 cm (3 in), then turn up another 7.5 cm (3 in) — on both the curtain fabric and lining fabric. The lining should be about 2 cm (¾ in) shorter than the curtain fabric. Make mock mitres at the corners of the curtain fabric hems. Pin and tack both hems.

10 Turn the curtains right side out again and press. Draw up the tape until it is the correct width and hang *in situ* for a few days to allow the fabric to 'drop'. Then, adust the hems if necessary and slipstitch. Slipstitch the lower side seam openings.

Making a pair of simple lined curtains with a bound edge

Curtains with a bound edge in a contrast colour look very jolly, are easy to make and are economical on fabric too. Choose a co-ordinating fabric for the lining, but not one so strongly patterned that it will show through on the front.

Measuring up

To work out the number of lengths of curtain fabric you need, multiply the width of the track by the fullness (i.e. 1½ or 2) then divide by the width of the fabric. Round up the nearest whole number. This is the number of lengths of fabric you will need.

To calculate the total amount of curtain fabric needed, measure from the hook suspension point on the track or pole (i.e. the small rings that the hooks go into) to the sill and add 3 cm (1¼ in), Multiply this measurement by the number of lengths required to calculate the total amount of fabric needed. You do not need to allow extra for seams. You need the identical amount of fabric for the lining.

You will need

Curtain fabric, calculated as above
Lining fabric, calculated as above
Sufficient 6 cm (2½ in) wide straight strips of plain contrast fabric to bind the edges of the curtains, joining them together to make up the length

1 Cut the curtain fabric and lining fabric, following steps 1-4 for unlined curtains. Make any necessary joins using 1.5 cm (⅝ in) open seams and press them open.

2 Repeat for the lining.

RIGHT SIDE
OF CURTAIN
FABRIC

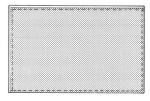

3 Lay the lining fabric on top of the curtain fabric, wrong sides together (i.e. right sides outwards) and raw edges level. Tack close to all raw edges.

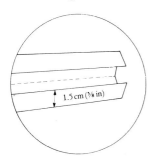

1.5 cm (⅝ in)

4 Cut a long enough piece of binding to go right the way round the curtain with a little extra over. Press the binding in half down the middle, open it up, then press the raw edges in so they meet the centre line.

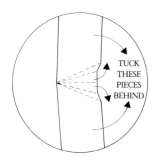

TUCK
THESE
PIECES
BEHIND

5 Pin the binding around the edge of the fabric, slotting the raw edge of the fabric right into the binding, and having the join in the binding coinciding with one of the

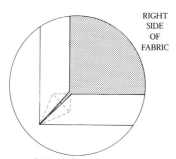

RIGHT
SIDE
OF
FABRIC

corners. Mitre the corners of the binding on both sides by tucking the central corner triangle of fabric inside.

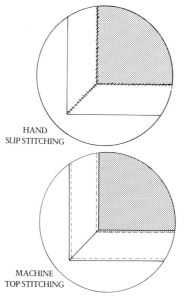

HAND
SLIP STITCHING

MACHINE
TOP STITCHING

6 Tack the binding in place, then either hand-stitch it in place with tiny slipstitches, or machine top-stitch close to both edges.

7 Apply the curtain tape as for unlined curtains steps 11–13.

Making a roller blind

A roller blind is not difficult to make, particularly if you use a kit, and it is very economical on fabric. Kits do not include fabric so you need to buy this too; instructions for measuring up are given below. Choose a plain fabric to co-ordinate with the colour scheme, or make a feature of a strongly patterned fabric. If you are feeling especially creative you can decorate a plain blind with fabric paints and stencils.

Choosing fabric
Choose wide fabrics to avoid joins. If there are seams in the fabric it will wind on to the roller unevenly, so on a wide window it is better to have more than one blind than to join fabric. Use specially treated roller blind fabric (holland), firm, closely woven cotton or cotton/polyester or PVC. Or you can stiffen fabric using a special spray (follow instructions carefully and work in a well-ventilated room). The spray may make the fabric shrink, so allow for this in your calculations and do not cut the fabric until after you have sprayed it. Allow an extra 1 cm (⅜ in) on each side for side seams if you are stiffening the fabric yourself.

Measuring up
Roller blinds can either be fitted close to the window frame or outside the window recess,

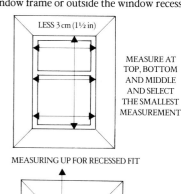

LESS 3 cm (1½ in)

MEASURE AT
TOP, BOTTOM
AND MIDDLE
AND SELECT
THE SMALLEST
MEASUREMENT

MEASURING UP FOR RECESSED FIT

MEASURING UP FOR SURFACE MOUNTING

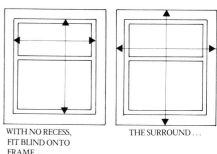

WITH NO RECESS,
FIT BLIND ONTO
FRAME . . .

THE SURROUND . . .

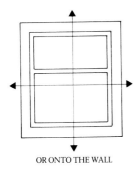

OR ONTO THE WALL

if there is one. If the frame is not wood and therefore impossible to drill into, the fixings can be mounted on to the wall surrounding the frame, or even into the ceiling. Decide where you intend to mount your blind, and measure the dimensions using a steel tape measure. For a blind that fits into the recess, measure the width of your window recess exactly, at the top, middle and bottom (in case the sides are not exactly parallel). Select the smallest measurement of the three and subtract 1.5 cm (⅝ in) at each side to allow for the roller pins and brackets. If a blind is going outside the recess or is for a window that has no recess, allow a bit extra all round 4–5 cm (1⅝–2 in) on the top, bottom and sides — to make sure that light will not show around the edges.

You will need

Fabric to the required size
Roller blind kit in the right size for the window
Thread
2.5 cm (1 in) wooden batten or lath the width of the blind less 1 cm (⅜ in)
Junior hacksaw to cut the roller and batten to length
Clear adhesive

1 Position the brackets on the window frame or surround, following the instructions supplied with the kit. If the

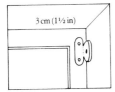

brackets are to be fixed into a recess, screw the brackets 3 cm (1¼ in) down from the top to allow for the thickness of the blind on the roller. There is usually a bracket with an angled slot in it that goes on the left, and one with a central hole in it that goes on the right. Measure between the brackets and calculate the roller length. Cut it to size if necessary.

2 Stiffen the fabric if necessary. Cut the fabric to the width of the roller by the length of the window, adding 15 cm (6 in) to the drop for turnings. You should not need side seams if the fabric is ready stiffened, but if you are stiffening it yourself allow an extra 1 cm (⅜ in) on each side for a side seam and zig-zag stitch it after stiffening. It is essential that the fabric is cut perfectly square, otherwise it will not wind on to the roller properly and it will not hang straight. Use a T-square or set-square to make sure all your corners are 90°.

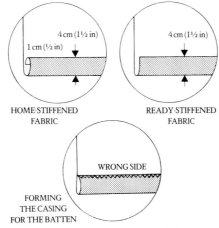

3 Turn the bottom edge 4 cm (1⅝ in) towards the wrong side and press it. If you have stiffened the fabric yourself, turn it

under another 1 cm (⅜ in) first. Avoid using pins to hold the fabric in place (these may leave holes in the fabric) — use transparent sticky tape instead — and machine zig-zag close to the raw edge to form a casing for the batten.

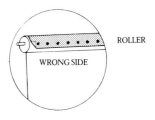

4 Follow the kit manufacturer's instructions for fixing the top edge of the fabric to the roller. Usually this is done using double-sided tape or tacks, with the wrong side of the fabric next to the roller. Make sure the fabric is square on to the roller — there is usually a guide-line on the roller to help you. Ensure when you attach the fabric that the spring mechanism is at the correct end (usually the left). You can tell which end this is supposed to be by looking at the brackets. The end with the spring in it rests in the slotted bracket.

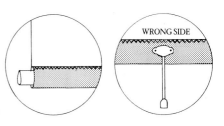

5 Cut the wooden batten 1 cm (⅜ in) shorter than the width of the blind, then slide it in the casing. Cut the pull cord to the right length, allowing a little extra for knots. Knot one end of it and slide the 'acorn' on to the cord to conceal the knot. Thread the other end of the knot into the cord fixing plate and knot it to hold it in place. Screw the plate to the back of the blind, into the centre point of the batten.

6 Hang the blind on its brackets. Tension the spring, if necessary, following the manufacturer's instructions.

Making a roman blind

Roman blinds give a very neat look to a window, and are very economical on fabric too. They are not difficult to make, provided you measure up carefully and keep your seams straight. Like roller blinds, they are good for showing off distinctive patterns because the fabric lies flat when the blinds are down. Window sizes vary so it is obviously not possible to give the actual measurements of materials you will need. Read through the instructions fully first and plan your blinds before you start to make them. Sketch out a set of diagrams, with the measurments marked on, for your own windows. That way you can calculate exactly how much of everything you will need.

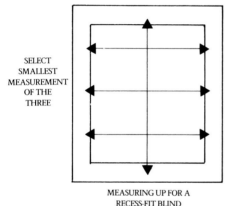

SELECT
SMALLEST
MEASUREMENT
OF THE
THREE

MEASURING UP FOR A
RECESS-FIT BLIND

Measuring up

Decide whether you want the blind to hang inside or outside the window recess. If inside, measure the width of your window recess at the top, middle and bottom (in case the sides are not exactly parallel). Deduct 1 cm (⅜ in) from the smallest measurement of the three, to arrive at the finished width of the blind. This allows clearance so the blind can rise and fall freely. If the blind is to hang outside the recess or on a frame with no recess, decide how wide your blind needs to be in order to cover the window without skimping. Allow about 4–5 cm (1⅝–2 in) extra on the top, bottom and sides to prevent light coming in round the edges. For diagrams refer to the 'measuring up' section for roller blinds.

For each blind you will need

Planed softwood, 5 × 2.5 cm (2 × 1 in) × the width of the blind
Saw
Emery paper
Paint or varnish
Brush
White spirit to clean up
Fabric
Lining fabric — choose a good quality light-proof fabric for preference
Sewing thread
Fine dowelling
A wooden lath 2 cm (¾ in) shorter than the softwood batten
Junior hacksaw
Small brass or nylon rings
Small flat-topped nails and a hammer, or a staple gun and staples
Small angle irons and screws, or long screws and Rawlplugs
Bradawl and/or electric drill
Fine nylon cord (see below for quantity)
Wooden or nylon acorn

1 Cut a piece of 5 × 2.5 cm (2 × 1 in) planed softwood to your width measurement and sand it down. Varnish or paint it to match the window frame's surround.
2 For the fabric width, add 9 cm (3¾ in) to the batten measurement (for turnings). For the length measure from the top of the window to the sill and add 13 cm (5¼ in) for the bottom hem and top fixing. When you calculate and cut your top fabric, take into account any obvious repeats. Motifs, for example, should be centred and if there is more than one blind for a window, the repeats should all be level. This may mean you will have to buy extra fabric.

A completely co-ordinated look can be achieved by stencilling on fabric, as well as on walls and furniture. Here a ready-cut design has been used creatively to get a range of different effects. Special fabric stencil paint has been used on the curtains and was fixed according to the manufacturer's instructions.

Roller blinds make a very neat and simple window treatment and roll right up out of the way when not in use. They also provide an inexpensive solution to storage problems: as shown here, a roller blind can hide the chaos of an untidy shelf unit. When you want to use the shelves the blind can be rolled up and, unlike a door, does not get in the way.

This particular design of made-to-measure blind has a special rubberized, light-proof backing which helps prevent small children waking at the crack of dawn. The blind can also be wiped over to remove sticky finger prints.

A strong pattern like this teddy bear design can provide the inspiration for a whole room scheme. Motifs, for example, can be used as inspiration for a stencil design, colours can be picked out and matched to paint and accessories.

3 Cut the lining to the same length as the top fabric, but 12 cm (5 in) narrower. You will also need some extra lining fabric for dowel casings (see step 7).

4 If your chosen top or lining fabrics are not wide enough to go across the width of the window you will need to join lengths of fabric. Remember to add 3 cm (1¼ in) to the width of fabric for every seam you have to make — this allows 1.5 cm (⅝ in) seams. Make sure any joins are either centred or equally spaced to either side of the centre line. Remember to match repeats. Press any seams open.

5 Lay your top fabric on the lining fabric, right sides facing. Pin the side seams together, with the raw side edges level. Machine 1.5 cm (⅝ in) in from the edge. Press the seam open and turn right side out, to form a tube. Press flat along the outside edges so a 2 cm (¾ in) margin of top fabric is formed on either side of the lining. Tack with big stitches along both centre lines to hold the lining and top fabric in place. At the bottom edge, turn the fabric and lining under 1 cm (⅜ in) towards the lined side and press. Turn under another 7.5 cm (3 in) to form a casing. Machine-stitch close to the folded edge.

6 Cut some more pieces of lining fabric 2 cm (¾ in) longer than your batten, by 5 cm (2 in). The number of strips you will need depends on the length of your blind. You will need one for every 20–25 cm (8–10 in) of drop, bearing in mind that the topmost and bottommost ones will be 20–25 cm (8–10 in) in from either end. Mark the long centre line of each strip with a pencil, tailor's chalk,

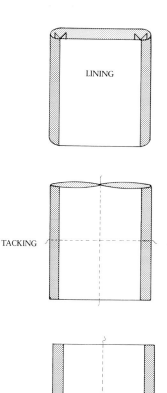

LINING

TACKING

BOTTOM CASING

FRONT FABRIC

LINING

pencil or vanishing cloth marker. Press 1 cm (⅜ in) turnings along the long edges and then 1 cm (⅜ in) on the short ends. Draw a line across the back of your blind every 20–25 cm (8–10 in), spaced evenly down the blind and leaving an even gap at the top and bottom. Pin a strip to every line on your blind, matching up the marked lines. Machine each strip in place along the line. Then fold each strip in half along the centre line and slip-stitch by hand or machine close to the folded long edges. Cut thin dowelling, with a junior hacksaw, 2 cm (¾ in) shorter than the batten width and slide a dowel into each of the pockets. Slip-stitch both ends. Cut the lath 2 cm (¾ in) shorter than the bottom casing. Slide it into the bottom casing and slip-stitch the ends. Take out tacking.

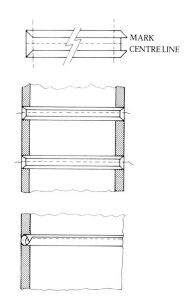

MARK CENTRE LINE

7 Sew small brass or nylon rings to the back of the blind, 2 cm (¾ in) in from each end of each dowel pocket. Unless you have a very narrow blind, add one or more rows in between. Space them out evenly, about 25–30 cm (10–12 in) apart, making sure the rings align vertically.

8 Fold 4.5 cm (1¾ in) of the top of the blind over the top of the batten. Fix in place using a staple gun, or small, flat-topped nails. Make sure the blind is exactly square to the batten or the blind will not hang straight. Screw eyes into the underside of the batten, lining one up with each of the rows of rings. Screw angle irons to the inside edge of the board where it will meet the window. If you have metal window frames you will have to fix the batten into the top of the reveal using long screws and Rawlplugs.

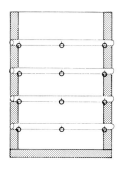

9 To calculate how much cord you need, measure the length of your blind, double it and multiply it by the number of rows of rings. To this measurement add the distance between the rows of rings, if you only have two rows. If you have three rows add on this measurement multiplied by three; if you have four rows add this measurement multiplied by six; if you have five rows add ten

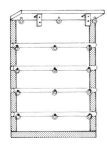

times the measurement. Cut off one piece of cord twice the length of the blind. Cut each successive piece as long as the one you cut before, but each time add on the distance between two rows, so each piece will be longer than the piece before. Continue like this until you have cut all the lengths — you should have one for each row of rings.

10 Fix the blind in place in the window. Take the shortest piece of cord. Tie one end of it to the bottom ring of the row nearest the side you want the cord to hang. Thread the cord up through the other rings in that vertical row, and then through the eye in the batten. Take the next longest piece of cord and tie it to the bottom ring of the next row, pass it up through that line of rings, through the

eye at the top and then across through the eye above the first row. If you have more than two rows of rings continue in this way, using the next longest piece, and so on. Remember as you take the cord across the top to thread it through all the previous top eyes.

11 When all the cords are hanging together at one side, thread an acorn on to the cords, knot them level with the sill, trim if necessary and pull the acorn down to cover the knot. Fix the cleat to a convenient place on the window frame or reveal (you will need Rawlplugs if you use the reveal) but high enough up so that it is out of reach of small fingers. When the blind is pulled up, wind the end of the cord around the cleat.

Creating your own fabric designs and patterns for curtains and blinds

You will need

Blind or curtains
Fabric paint or stencil paint
Synthetic sponge or stencil brushes for stencilling
Masking tape or vanishing cloth marker

Just as it is quite simple to stencil or paint your own designs on the walls, it is no more complicated to stencil or paint on fabric. Blinds in particular are a good surface for decorating because they are flat and therefore the design is shown off to its best advantage. If you have stencilled a frieze round the room, for example, you can continue it across the blind so that when the blind is down it completes the design.

Once you have chosen the stencil design (see Chapter 2 for how to design and cut stencils) you will need to plan where the motifs are to be positioned on the blind or curtain. Masking tape is useful for providing guide-lines which are very easy to remove. A vanishing cloth marker is an alternative and provides more accurate lines, but test it on a part of the fabric that will not show before you go ahead.

The type of paint that you use will depend on the surface you are working on. If you are stencilling on to curtains then you will need to use fabric stencilling paint, so that you can wash the fabric. Follow the manufacturer's instructions for fixing the dye (this usually involves ironing it). If you are stencilling on blinds, which will have been stiffened and will not be washed, then you should use specialist stencilling paint.

If possible, experiment on a scrap piece of fabric first (see Chapter 2 for stencilling techniques). Remember that, unlike stencilling with paint, it is not possible to cover over mistakes: when working on the real thing you must get it right first time. So err on the side of caution and apply only a little colour at a time and as dryly as possible to avoid drips and runs. You can always work over it again to boost the colour.

Whether working on curtains or blinds, make sure you have enough space to spread them out flat and check you have a firm surface underneath when stencilling. If you are working on lined curtains you will need to put a sheet of plastic between the curtain and its lining to prevent paint seeping on to the lining. Place some absorbent paper on top of the plastic to prevent paint spreading on the back of the work. Leave the blind or curtain out flat until it is completely dry. Be especially careful not to roll a roller blind up until you are absolutely sure it is dry.

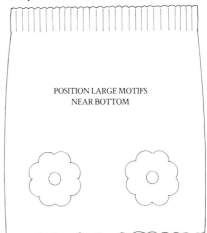

POSITION LARGE MOTIFS NEAR BOTTOM

Large designs on curtains and blinds should have whole motifs near the bottom as shown.

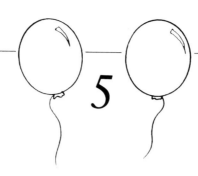

5

LIGHTING, HEATING AND BABY ALARMS

Lighting tends to be the least considered part of a room scheme, and this is particularly true of babies' and children's rooms. Yet outside daylight hours, lighting possibly has more impact on the appearance of a room, its comfort and its usefulness than any other single factor. Lighting plays a very big role in making a room scheme look its best plus, if well planned, lighting can make practical tasks a whole lot simpler and more pleasurable.

PLANNING THE CORRECT LIGHTING

So if you are thinking of having any rewiring done in your child's room, it is worth taking a little extra time to plan the lighting carefully. A child's room is used more, and for a greater variety of uses, than an adult bedroom so it needs a really adaptable lighting scheme. Bear in mind too that you will frequently be turning the light on in the middle of the night, so it makes life much more pleasant if the lighting in the room is efficient yet subtle and atmospheric, rather than glaring and harsh.

Lighting is divided up into three basic types — general lighting, task lighting and accent lighting — each of which fulfils a different purpose. General lighting gives overall illumination to a room. Task lighting provides light for specific needs, and makes carrying out certain activities and jobs easier. Accent lighting is for decorative rather than practical purposes and gives local rather than overall illumination. In a child's room this would mean lights directed at pictures,

murals, posters or shelves. Since this type of lighting could be regarded as a luxury, it is the one to leave out if your budget is tight. Fittings can also be combined for economy — a fitting such as a row of spotlights that provides task lighting for changing nappies can also provide general lighting.

General lighting

Usually the general lighting in a room comes from a pendant light hanging from the centre of the ceiling. This is the sort of lighting that most houses are fitted with as standard, but it is not the ideal way to light a room as the effect is invariably harsh, dismal and unfriendly. It is particularly unsuitable for a baby, who will be lying in his cot staring straight up into the light fitting. If you are unwilling or unable to change a central ceiling pendant then use a large decor bulb, or a large translucent shade which hides the bulb, in order to diffuse the light as much as possible.

Wall lights are better than pendants — the best ones throw the light up on to the ceiling and bounce it back down into the room, giving a soft yet efficient light. Plaster, bowl-shaped fittings that you paint yourself are particularly good as the bulb and inner workings of the fitting are concealed from the baby's view. The plaster bowl can be decorated to match the room scheme and can be repainted over and over again. If you opt for this type of fitting you will probably need at least two (more if it is a large room), as the light they give off is fairly soft. Also, point a torch up the wall to check that there are no bumps in it which will be emphasized by such a fitting. If there are, either get the wall replastered or consider another type of fitting. Bulkhead lights on the wall provide good general lighting for boisterous older children. The unit is sealed, robust, available in bright colours and gives a jolly, hi-tech look to a room.

Alternatively you could consider two or

three spotlights on a track, which can usually be fitted in place of the pendant. Track lighting is very versatile and can be angled on to pictures, posters or favourite toys, providing accent lighting as well. By angling the fittings on to the wall the light bounces off the wall and into the room, giving a more pleasant effect than fittings pointing directly into the room. Spotlights are also available as individual fittings which can be dotted around the room.

Recessed downlighters are another

alternative. 'Eyeball' fittings are particularly useful as they can be angled towards the wall to give a softer effect. Downlighters are set into holes in the ceiling so are only suitable if you have a sufficiently deep ceiling void. Check before you buy that you have enough clearance, and also bear in mind that the positioning of these types of lights will be restricted by the layout of the ceiling joists and any pipe work immediately above the ceiling. Do not install one of these fittings above your child's cot or bed, though, or it

Spotlights mounted on beams are a perfect way to light this spacious attic playroom. They provide efficient lighting on the floor area for playing, and give accent lighting for the end wall with its shelving units. The fittings themselves are discreet and, while being a very practical lighting solution, the overall effect is subtle.

The cork tiles are also a very practical choice of flooring, offering warmth, resilience, ease of cleaning, durability and also an excellent surface for toy cars!

will shine straight into his eyes.

Whichever type of general lighting you choose, you should consider replacing the wall switch with a dimmer. This will allow you to turn the light on very low for night-time feeds, or to check up on your child at night without disturbing him. It also means that if you do have to turn the light on full in the middle of the night for some reason you can turn it on gradually without startling the baby. A dimmer also allows the main room light to be used as a night light. Always check when you buy a fitting that it is suitable for use with a dimmer as a few types are not.

Task lighting

In a baby's room, task lighting will initially be some sort of fitting to enable you to see what you are doing when changing nappies and dressing your child, and should be above the work surface where you carry this out. It could be in the form of a downlighter, pendant light, spotlight or wall light, preferably dimmable or fitted with a low wattage bulb so as not to be too bright for the baby's eyes. Whatever you choose should be out of the child's reach. Later on your child will need light for writing and drawing at his desk, so choose a fitting which will act as a task light for this sort of activity. A fitting that is out of the child's reach, such as a wall-mounted spotlight, is safer and takes up no desk space.

You will be reading to your child in bed so you will need some kind of bedside lighting even before he learns to read. This must be a stable fitting that the child cannot reach, such as a wall-mounted spotlight or a bulkhead light. Later the child will need a pull cord or switch that he can operate near the bed so he will not have to find his way across the room in the dark after turning off the room light. Never fix clip-on spotlights close to or on to part of the bed. Even with older children who understand and respect electricity, such fittings can come adrift and fall on to bedding, and if switched on could overheat and cause a fire.

Many children reach a stage when they are afraid of the dark, so some form of low lighting can be a great comfort to a child if he wakes up in the night. As mentioned before, this can take the form of a dimmed room light. Night lights are also available in novelty shapes which can look very attractive. Be sure that your child does not think it is a toy, though, and make sure any night light you choose is tip-resistant. Some night lights come complete with plug-in transformers which reduce the voltage to a safe 12v and some have built-in dimmers.

If you choose a free-standing lamp for your baby's room make sure the flex is neatly tucked away so nobody can trip over it. Do not run flex under a carpet where people can tread on it as the wire can become worn without you noticing and cause a fire. Always keep free-standing lights well away from your baby's cot so he cannot reach them, and once he starts to crawl put any lamps away until he is old enough to know not to tug on the flex and pull them over.

Glowing lights are also available that fit straight into a plug socket, offering soft light at floor level. Some plug lights have a light-sensitive switch so they turn on during the night and off at daybreak — thus saving electricity. Once children are old enough to find their way to the bathroom during the night, it is useful to have plug-in glow lights along the hallway and in other dark areas.

Safety first

When you are dealing with a small child's room the foremost consideration must be safety, so do be sure that any fittings are safe for the child at that particular stage in his development and that you position them safely too. Never attempt electrical work yourself unless you really do know what you are doing. If you are in any doubt at all call in a competent, qualified electrician.

Lighting safety points

○ Err on the side of caution as far as electricity is concerned because children do not understand the dangers involved.
○ Keep fittings out of the reach of children until you are sure they will not burn themselves on them, knock them over or tamper with them.

○ Never exceed the maximum bulb wattages recommended by manufacturers for their fittings.
○ Only buy electrical goods from reliable, reputable companies and avoid cheap imports which may not meet government standards.
○ Look for government safety symbols on fittings.
○ Some fittings are very attractive and designed with children in mind — if you choose this type make sure they are well out of the reach of children until they are old enough to respect electricity. Do not encourage your child to think of them as a sort of toy.
○ Use moulded or unbreakable safety plugs with the correct fuse for the appliance. For lamps this will usually be 3 amps.
○ Check that your plug sockets are the modern shuttered type. If not, get them replaced by a qualified electrician.

Planning a lighting scheme

Rewiring should be done before you decorate, so to save money and subsequent upheaval it is advisable to work out what is likely to be needed in the future and have all the work done at once. Make a list of all the uses to which the room might be put in the future and try to visualize where electrical equipment (such as desk lamps, plug-in spot lights, televisions, heaters and computers) may be used so extra plug sockets can be installed in one go.

Draw up a plan of the room on graph paper with 1 cm equalling 50 cm (or 1 in equalling 20 in). Mark on plug sockets, existing light fittings and the position of furniture. Write on the plan which jobs take place where or which jobs are likely to take place there in the future (e.g. nappy changing, homework, reading in bed, etc.). Mark in where you need extra lighting and decide which will be the best sort of fittings for the purpose.

Also decide where you need extra plug sockets. If possible, have the sockets positioned out of reach of crawling babies and toddlers or use plastic socket covers until the child is old enough to respect electricity.

HEATING

Whether your baby is going to sleep in with you for the time being, or whether he will have a room of his own, it is important that the room is kept at the right temperature both day and night. This is particularly important for the first 4–6 weeks as a young baby does not move around very much and cannot regulate his body temperature. Recent research has shown that babies do not need hot rooms – around 18°C (65°F) is ideal – and that overheating has been shown to play a part in cot death. So make sure that there is adequate ventilation and invest in a simple wall thermometer.

You only need all-night heating in cold weather. Many homes today have central heating systems with a time switch to turn the heating off at night. In order to leave the heating on only in the baby's room you will have to turn all the other radiators off and override the timer. Having individual thermo-stats on radiators makes easier work of this.

Radiators are usually positioned under windows because cooler air coming in through the glass sets up a convection current which circulates air around the room. However if you are installing a radiator in the nursery and are trying to decide where it should be sited, bear in mind that if you put a radiator in the middle of a wall you will be limited as to what you can subsequently do with that part of the room. Do not put your baby's cot next to the radiator.

Even with central heating there may be times when an extra heater is useful, especially if your radiators do not have individual thermostats. Even if they do, you probably will not want your central heating on all the time and having a separate heater can work out more economically in the long run.

Convection heaters

There are several types of heater to choose from, and some are more suitable for children's rooms than others. Bear in mind that there are two types of heat, convected

heat and radiant heat, and heaters work on one or other of these principles, or occasionally combine the two. The first choice of heater for a nursery is a wall-mounted, thermostatically controlled convection heater. Convection heaters work by heating air over hot elements, and the air then rises gently through the top grills. Then it cools, sinks, and is drawn in through the bottom of the heater, and the cycle starts again.

Because convector heaters rely on a warm air current to work, they must be positioned as near the floor as possible. However, free-standing heaters are not suit-able for use in children's rooms, so always use wall-mounted models. Look for extra features such as a timer which allows you to set the heater to come on in advance and have the room warmed up ready for you, and an automatic cut-out should the air vents accidently become covered or blocked.

Fan heaters are a form of convector heater with the addition of a fan to speed up the convection process. This type of heater is excellent for heating rooms rapidly and very efficiently but, unlike ordinary convectors, they create a noticeable blast of hot air and most of them make some noise. This means they are better when used for short periods of time rather than continuously, making them less suitable for use in a nursery than an ordinary convector heater. Again, if you do choose this type it must be wall-mounted, but because fans direct the heat they can be positioned anywhere on the wall.

Radiant heaters

Radiant heat is the same type of heat as the sun's. There is usually a red-hot bar in fires that use this principle, and there may also be a reflector to direct the heat. If used in a nuresery this type of heater must always be mounted high up on the wall. Radiated heat travels in a straight line without heating the air it passes through. Instead, it warms the walls and objects in the room which in turn

warm the air, so the closer you are to the fire, the warmer you will be. Although radiant heaters are slightly more efficient than convectors, they are not really suitable for nurseries as their effect is harsh. Convector heaters give a much more comfortable room temperature and a more cosy effect.

Because both convected and radiated heat have their advantages and disadvantages a combination is best, although this is found in only a few types of heater. Oil-filled radiators are one, and although they are not particularly economical they are quiet, give comfortable, constant heat and are much simpler to install than central heating. The oil never needs changing and there are no moving parts so they are very reliable. Column designs are particularly efficient although more compact, slimline versions are also available. Some models also feature built-in timers, some of which allow you to set different daily heating requirements over a seven-day cycle. An override switch allows you to use the heater whenever you wish without affecting the timer settings. If you choose an oil-filled radiator for a nursery, always have it fixed to the wall.

Safety with heaters

○ Whichever type you choose must be safe (i.e. approved by a recognized safety board) — remember you must be able to leave your child alone in the room with the heater. Go to a reputable dealer and choose a reputable make. Never be tempted to buy second-hand.

○ Apart from central heating radiators, never fit heaters under or near windows if they could get covered or blocked by curtains, and never hang washing over heaters or cover them up in any way.

○ Paraffin heaters, gas fires, electric bar fires (with the exception of wall-mount-ed models fitted high up on the wall) are not suitable for use in nurseries.

○ If a heater needs installing, call in a qualified expert unless you do really

know what you are doing. Electric heaters should be securely fixed in place and permanently wired into fused connection units.

However, even an ordinary radiator could burn a child if, for example, he tried to pull himself up or climb on it. Radiators tend to be placed under windows, and that is where a child often wants to climb to look out, do not have the thermostat turned up too high. Once the child is crawling, leave a towel draped over the radiator or, as a more permanent solution, you can buy a radiator cover. As radiators are often not particularly attractive either, a radiator cover improves the look of the room. Bear in mind that there must be access to the valves and for bleeding trapped air but check that the holes in the front of the cover are not so small that your child could trap his fingers.

BABY ALARMS

A baby listener is very useful and enables you to get on with something in another room, once you have put your child in his cot, without having to strain to listen out for him. The transmitter part is in your child's room and the receiver is placed in the room you are occupying. Some baby listeners are two-way and allow you to talk reassuringly to your child without having to go to his room. Some have portable receivers which clip on to your belt so you can move around the house or even go into the garden.

There is also a plug-in type which operates through the mains wiring in your home. You plug one unit into a mains socket in your child's room and one in the room you are occupying, and you will be able to hear your

As radiators are not often all that attractive despite often visually dominating a room, a radiator grille can smarten up the look of a room considerably. In a child's room, such a fitting has the additional advantage of preventing the child from getting near a hot radiator.

child. The advantages are that you can move the sockets around to any room in the house and you can take them with you when you go away.

Whichever type of baby listener you choose, always make sure the baby end of the alarm is out of your child's reach, and do not rely on it completely. Children can get themselves into trouble without making any noise, so still check up on your child from time to time.

6

FURNITURE AND STORAGE

SLEEPING ARRANGEMENTS

When your baby is first born you can put him straight into a cot, but most parents prefer to use something smaller first, such as a Moses basket, carry-cot or crib, which is cosier for the child and makes him feel more secure. You will need special bedding for this, although you can also make use of it in the pram (see Chapter 7). A crib, although it looks very pretty, is a bit of a luxury, because it can only be used for a few months.

Moses baskets

If you want something pretty which is less expensive, you can use a Moses basket. These baskets are easily transportable (check that the handles are firmly secured) and are available with ready-made frills and lining. The lining should be detachable and in easy-care fabric so it can be removed and washed. You can always use the basket for storing things in later. It can be used with a stand, although you must make sure that the basket fits well and cannot tip over, or alternatively you can put the basket in a cot. A Moses basket is, however, only suitable for a very young baby. You must transfer him to a cot well before he can push himself up on his arms or sit up, which will probably be when he is between three and six months old.

Carry-cots

An alternative to a Moses basket or crib is a carry-cot or pram top. These are not as pretty, but are very practical because they are easy to move around (check that the handles are correctly placed so that the carry-cot does not tip over when you pick it up) and can also be combined with a transporter or a pram base, and used as a pram. Indoors they can be used on a stand, and some stands double up for use as a baby bath stand. If you place a carry-cot on a stand, the stand should not be less than three-quarters of the length of the carry-cot, and should be wider than it to make sure it is completely stable. Also check when you buy that it is designed to take the weight of carry-cot that you are going to use with it.

On the minus side, carry-cots may be plastic-lined, which makes some babies too hot, so you may wish to borrow one and try it out before you buy. Avoid a carry-cot with a very soft plastic lining which might interfere with your baby's breathing should he roll against it.

Choosing a cot

Even if you did not put your baby in a cot straight away, you will need one once he is a few months old. It is important to choose a cot that is well-made, safe and sturdy and which conforms to recommended safety standards. If you decide to use a second-hand one, be sure it conforms to current standards. If it does not, you should replace it with one that does.

A cot should have high sides and ends so that the baby cannot climb out, and the minimum distance between the base of the mattress and the top of the cot should be 59.5 cm (23¾ in). All the bars should be vertical, so that a child cannot climb up them like a ladder — this even means that cots with horizontal rows of beads set into the bars are unsuitable, since the child could use them as a foot-hold to climb out. The spaces between the bars of the cot should be no less than 2.5 cm (1 in) and not more than 6 cm (2½ in), so the child can neither squeeze out between the bars, nor get parts of his body trapped between them.

Most cots have an adjustable drop-side mechanism so it is easy to make the bed and lift the baby in and out. The fastening mechanism should operate automatically, be safe and designed in such a way that it is impossible for the child to lower the side on his own. Older cots may have mechanisms with protruding parts on which a child can catch his clothes and injure or strangle himself, so examine second-hand cots very carefully.

Some cots also have an adjustable base height which can be used in the highest position when the child is too young to sit up. This allows you to tuck in the baby without having to bend down or lower the side. Once the child becomes more active you can lower the base to the lower, safer level.

A cot should also be finished with non-toxic paint or varnish and should have no decorative transfers on the inside (these can flake off and be swallowed) or peeling paint. If you have a second-hand cot and have no way of knowing whether the finish contains lead or not, strip off all the paint or varnish and repaint or varnish it with non-toxic materials.

Apart from the standard type of cot, some cots are available with drawers underneath, and some also have cupboards on the end. It is also possible to buy separate drawers on castors which will slip under most designs of cot. These drawers can be used later for toy storage. Cot beds are also available which convert into a small bed suitable for a child up to about six years old. After that some designs can be used as a sofa. Cot beds only really make sense if you are having just one child, otherwise you will need another cot for the second baby.

Mattresses for cots will either be sprung or made from combustion modified foam. A foam mattress will be cheaper, but a sprung mattress will last longer. If you buy a foam mattress make sure it is a safety design with ventilation holes at the head end. Mattresses should carry a label to show the size of cot they are intended for (a new cot should also have a label to tell you which size of mattress will fit it). Getting the size right is important because a mattress must fit a cot well, with no gaps at the sides or ends where arms or legs could get trapped. You should really only be able to insert a finger between the mattress and the edge of the cot, so allowing you just enough space to tuck in the bedding. Cot mattresses should not be fitted with handles, since a child could trap his arms or legs in them.

Choosing a bed

Once a child is about two he will be ready to graduate to a bed. Never give a child a second-hand bed. Not only is it unhygenic but the bed will already have been moulded to someone else's shape, and that is bad for a growing child's development. Because a child does most of his growing in bed, it makes sense to buy the best quality bed you can afford. If space permits, invest in a bed that is 100 cm (40 in) wide, as children tend to move about in their sleep more than adults. Also, do not expect a bed to last forever. The life of a bed is about ten to fifteen years, so you should be prepared to replace it when the child is in his early teens.

When choosing a bed for a child it is important not to confuse a soft bed with a saggy one and draw the conclusion that a very firm bed is the best buy or will be good for your child's back (a so-called orthopaedic bed is really only a firm bed). Whether a person needs a firm or soft bed depends on their weight: a heavy person needs a firm bed to support them, a very light person needs a much softer bed. A bed has to support the small of its occupant's back and a firm bed is too hard to do that for a small child.

Take your child with you when you choose his bed. Get him to lie out flat on the bed, with a pillow. Slide your hand, palm downwards, under the small of his back. If there is a gap, the bed is too hard; if you have difficulty sliding your hand under then it is too soft; but if your hand slides under fairly easily but without there being a gap, the bed is about right and will offer the support your child needs. As long as you do not buy a cheap product, a soft or medium bed will be better for child's back, be more comfortable and should not become saggy. But to help the bed do its job properly, do not let your child bounce on it or use it as a trampoline.

Choosing a mattress

There are three types of mattress fillings used for beds: open springs, pocket springs and foam. Of the two types of sprung mattress, open springs are cheaper and, being bigger than pocket springs, give less precise support. However, a good quality open sprung mattress is comfortable and is perfectly adequate. But if you wish to spend more, a pocket sprung mattress will offer extra comfort and support.

If your child suffers from allergies such as asthma and hay fever, a foam mattress is the answer, because foam is hypoallergenic and does not harbour dust in the way that sprung mattresses do. However, if you do opt for a foam mattress, only buy the very best quality. Such mattresses often have ventilation holes running through them which eliminate the 'overheating' complaint that is often levelled at foam. What is more, cheap foam will not last and does not offer the support your child needs.

Always buy a mattress with the base intended for it, and do not try to economize by buying a new mattress for an old base (unless it is to go with a slatted wooden base, in which case you will need a special mattress). Even if the base looks all right the mattress will wear out that much more quickly and the mattress guarantee will be invalidated. A sprung-edge divan base is worth considering because it makes the bed comfortable right up to the edges, and protects the sides of the mattress.

If you have an attractive old bedstead which you want to use in your child's room it will probably be too saggy to provide decent support in its original state. If you really do want to use it you should seriously consider having a custom-made sprung base constructed which slots into the bed-well and rests on the side and end rails, although this is a fairly expensive proposition. Otherwise you really should forego the aesthetics and provide your child with a new divan bed instead.

Beds with storage space

While you are choosing a bed for your child, you may like to consider buying a type that either offers extra storage space, or which can sleep another child. There are two types of storage divan: one which has drawers in the side and one where the whole of the top of the bed lifts up. The second type is not suitable for children, and if you opt for the drawer divan make sure there is enough space in the room to open the drawers. Also bear in mind that drawer divan bases do not have as much room for springs as the ordinary type; they either have a solid top or a layer of very squat springs, both of which result in a very firm bed which may not be suitable for a small child.

Multiple beds

Truckle or stacking beds are very useful if your child often has friends to stay, or if your child's room has to double as the guest room. These beds come in various designs, but basically the idea is that one bed is concealed under the other and some designs push together to form a double bed. Bunk beds are another way to provide extra accommodation, although children under six should not sleep in them. If your child is younger, you could always remove the ladder and use the top bunk for storage or use only the bottom bunk, assembling when the child is older. Bear in mind before you decide on bunk beds that there are many accidents every year involving children and bunks so be sure that your children understand the dangers involved. If your country has government regulations and standards governing bunks, be sure that yours conforms to the most stringent rules whether it be new, second-hand or imported. The gap between slats and guard rails on the top bunk should be between 6 and 7.5 cm (2½–3 in); there should be guard rails on both sides of the top bunk and the access gap between the rails should be between 30–40 cm (12–16 in). If the bunks separate into two halves then they must have a secure fixing mechanism.

Also, be sure that any bunk bed you buy is supplied with decent mattresses — bunks often have cheap, thin foam mattresses — and that the height between the upper and lower bunk is sufficient to sit up in bed and also for an adult to sit on the bed to read a story.

FURNITURE AND STORAGE

As with everything else in the nursery, the furniture and storage that you choose should not only look good but, more importantly, should be practical and safe. You will need lots of storage space for all those things that babies and children need and accumulate, and it makes sense to choose furniture that can be made to look different as the years go by and that will last well into the teens and even into adulthood.

Initially, a baby's clothes tend to be folded up rather than hung up, so hanging space is less of a priority than drawer space. If you do have hanging rails these should be moved down to the lower half of the wardrobe space so once the child is a bit older he can help choose his clothes and tidy them away easily. Shelves can be fitted above the rail and can be removed when the child is older. A work-top area is useful for changing the baby (with plenty of storage space nearby for toiletries and nappies). At a later date this area can be used as a desk or dressing table, so it is useful if the work top has a knee-hole underneath. A bedside cabinet is also very useful. The top should be big enough so it can eventually take a lamp, a clock, books and comics, a drink and perhaps a radio.

Specially designed, small-scale children's storage is very charming but it makes more practical sense to opt for something larger from the start. Durable designs with easy-clean finishes make most sense, but remember that in the initial stages the furniture is just as much for your benefit as for your child's, so choose pieces that help make your job easier too.

If you are going to feed your baby in his room, you will need a comfortable chair. Traditionally, a nursing chair (as it is known) is a low, upholstered chair with a high back that offers you good support. You can, of course, choose any chair so long as it is comfortable and the arms are low enough to give you sufficient elbow room.

Bedroom storage, regardless of whether it is for adults or children, comes in three basic types: built-in furniture, free-standing furniture, and system furniture which is free-standing but has a fitted look. Built-in furniture is best because it makes the most economical use of floor space. You can utilize all the space between the floor and the ceiling, if you want to, and therefore it gives you the maximum storage for the minimum amount of floor area.

Built-in furniture

You could ask a local carpenter to construct built-in cupboards and wardrobes for you, you could build them yourself using wardrobe door units from hardwear stores, or you could go to specialist companies who supply and fit made-to-measure storage from a selection of ranges and designs. Whichever you choose, never buy just from a catalogue or glossy brochure. Make sure you see the finished article in a showroom or somebody's home, so you can check that it is sufficiently durable and is exactly what you and your child need.

Built-in furniture is also useful for straightening up an odd-shaped room because the storage is built to fit the room and can easily screen off alcoves and odd corners. As children are often given small or odd-shaped rooms, built-in storage makes a particularly good choice. Built-in furniture is also very stable, which makes it very safe in a room where toddlers may use furniture to pull themselves up, or for climbing on.

Another advantage of built-in storage is that you can often decide on the internal arrangements, such as the proportions of hanging space to shelf space, the heights of the rails and so on. If you can calculate everything that is likely to be kept in the room, you can then work out the most suitable arrangement. Always err on the side of generosity when deciding on how much storage you need.

If there is a completely clear wall in the room with no radiators, doors or windows this will provide an excellent position for lots

A hand basin in the corner of a child's room is an extremely useful addition. The plain white vanitory unit and tiles have been made into a co-ordinating feature simply by sticking a matching wallpaper border to the door panels and around the edges of the splash-back. This makes much simpler work of changing the overall look than when patterned tiles are used since you are not then committed to any one particular design or colourway.

The cupboard provides additional useful storage space for towels and other toilet articles and is fitted with a safety catch to deter prying fingers. If you do fit a hand basin into a child's room it is best to fit waterproof flooring material, such as vinyl or lino, in the area to protect the floor from splashes.

The wallpaper, an attractive all-over duck design, is complemented by its co-ordinating border. This border emphasizes the yellow in the wallpaper and brings a warm, bright and contrasting colour into what would otherwise be a predominantly blue room scheme. The successful use of a border partway round the room shows that a frieze can be included in the decor, even where a sloping ceiling might be thought to rule it out. A name picture, specially made for the room's occupant, also makes a child feel very special. The name has been spelt out in full, and under each letter has been painted an object that also begins with that letter of the alphabet. If you feel such a project would be beyond you, consider using cut-out letters and pictures from comics and magazines to create a name-collage.

Built-in, versatile storage, and lots of it, is probably the best choice for a child's room. It makes maximum use of the wall space between floor and ceiling and even utilizes awkward spaces, such as the areas under the sloping ceiling in this room. The plain white range shown here is ideal because it will blend in with almost any room scheme (you can easily change the door knobs to fit in with another colour scheme if necessary) and is just as appropriate for a baby as for a teenager. The work top in front of the window, for example, can be used as a nappy changing surface and later can become a desk for homework or a dressing table.

Co-ordinating bedlinen and curtains are the inspiration for the wall stencils which are used to create a border and also an all-over design. Part of the border design is also used to create a bed-head effect.

Safety note: As a small child could use this work top to gain access to the window, it would be advisable to fit vertical bars, or at least window locks, to a window in this sort of situation during a child's early years.

of built-in storage. However, you do not have to opt for a continuous run of wardrobes or cupboards. You may wish to have a break in the units to take the cot, and later the bed, or to break the run with a chest of drawers or a desk/dressing table unit with a knee-hole which can be used in the early stages as a changing unit.

Plain, flush doors are a good choice for children's rooms because they can be used for displaying posters or can even have a mural painted on them if the doors have a suitable surface (such as wood or hardboard; melamine or plasticized surfaces are difficult to paint on). In very small rooms you should consider sliding doors. They do not need clearance for opening, but they do have the disadvantage that the cupboard can never be opened completely; avoid cheap sliding door mechanisms as they may jam.

However, built-in storage can be costly and if you are intending to move in the near future you are unlikely to get your money back, although it may make your home easier to sell. A very inexpensive way to create built-in storage is to build simple shelves and hanging-rails and cover the front with jolly roller blinds or curtains to hide the chaos. If your child is particularly boisterous this may not be a good idea as he could swing on the curtains or play with the blinds and break the mechanism. If you think this is going to be a problem, you can always take the blinds down until he can be trusted not to damage them and just leave the storage unit open for the time being.

System furniture

The second type of bedroom storage systems, those that have a more-or-less fitted look but which are actually made up of units, are usually considerably less expensive than built-in ranges, yet they can be almost as space-efficient. Some companies actually make this type of furniture to measure (in which case it is comparable in price to built-in ranges), but mostly the furniture is off-the-peg and self-assembly.

Self-assembly wardrobes can, however, be quite a job to put together, as the panels are large and unwieldly. Always enlist the aid of

somebody else to help you. Like built-in systems, do not just buy from a catalogue or brochure. You will need this furniture to last and to stand up to hard wear, so it is important that you can see what sort of finish the furniture has, whether the hinges look strong, whether the drawers are sturdy and easy to slide in and out, and so on. This type of furniture is often designed to be bolted together and to the wall. It is particularly important that this is carried out, because children may try to clamber over pieces of furniture.

Free-standing furniture

This is the traditional choice for children's rooms, and has three main advantages: it can be the most inexpensive way to furnish rooms, it can be moved around (this is important consideration if you are planning to move house soon) and it can also be added to over the years. However, it is, as mentioned before, less economical on space than the other types of furniture and leaves less of the floor area free for playing. It is very important too that this type of furniture is solid and stable, and if necessary bolted to the wall to prevent accidents.

Second-hand furniture can be a good, economical choice for a child's room. Even if you choose pieces that do not really match, it is not too difficult to create a unified look by stripping the furniture, restoring it and giving all the pieces the same finish and all the same types of handle, for example. Again, if you are in any doubt about whether the paint or varnish on second-hand furniture is toxic, you should strip and repaint or varnish it anyway.

If you opt for free-standing furniture, do not clutter the room with lots of pieces of furniture to begin with, or it will obstruct valuable floor space. You will probably find that a wardrobe or tallboy, plus a chest of drawers (which can double as a changing surface), a toy chest (look for designs which have a special 'stay' to avoid trapping small fingers) and some shelves will offer more than enough storage to be going on with. If you need more furniture subsequently, then you can always add extra pieces.

Shelving

Whatever type of furniture you have chosen for your child's room, open shelving is a very useful addition. Initially it is useful for storing toys, later it can be used for books. Remember that children's picture books are often quite large so the shelves need to be fairly deep. As you will probably want to encourage your child to tidy up after himself, the shelving should be low enough for the child to reach. Make sure you do not put anything heavy on a higher shelf, as the child may pull it down on top of himself and do not put anything up so high that the child may put himself in danger by trying to reach it.

You can make your own shelving and fit it to the wall using battens or angle brackets, you can buy ready-made shelf units (you will probably have to assemble them yourself) or you can use an adjustable steel shelving system with brackets. Adjustable shelving makes most sense because it is flexible and, provided you buy a strong enough design to begin with (adjustable shelving systems vary in strength considerably), it can be used later on to house televisions, hi-fis and other weighty items. But whichever type of shelving you opt for, make sure the shelves are fixed firmly in position and, in the case of shelving units, that they are firmly fixed to the wall. For safety's sake, only buy an adjustable shelving system if there is provision for screwing the shelves firmly to the brackets.

Hanging shelves with adjustable steel brackets

Before you drill into the wall, use an electronic pipe and cable detector (these are not expensive and are a worthwhile investment) to check that there is nothing behind the wall that you should not drill into. As shelving is only as strong as the screws holding it to the wall, it is important to use the right fixings and to hang the uprights securely and properly. Check in the shop that you are buying the right fittings for your needs. For solid walls use suitable screws and wall plugs, for hollow partition walls choose either special cavity wall fixings, if the shelves are only to take light loads, or for heavier loads screw the uprights into the wooden uprights ('studs') behind the plasterboard. Locate these by knocking on the wall (it will sound dull where the studs are) and drilling into the wall to check you are working in the right place.

Measuring up

Shelf supports should be 50-80 cm (20-32 in) apart (any more than this and the shelves will sag), and the ends of shelves should not extend more than 20 cm (8 in) beyond the last bracket. Following these recommendations, work out how many uprights you need. Decide how many shelves you will need and how far apart they should be: from this you can calculate how long the uprights should be. Calculate the depth of the shelves, then work out how long the brackets should be. The brackets should be almost as long as the shelves are deep.

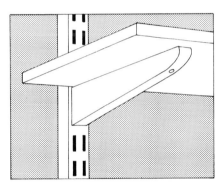

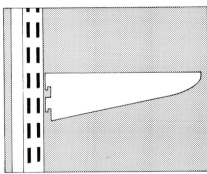

You will need

An electric drill (drill bit size will be specified on the fixings packet)
Shelf uprights

Masking tape
Shelf brackets (you will need a bracket for each shelf multiplied by the number of uprights)
Suitable wall fixings i.e. screws and plugs; these are often sold as kits by the shelving manufacturer
A spirit level
An expanding steel tape measure
Shelving: MDF (medium density fibreboard) or melamine-coated chipboard

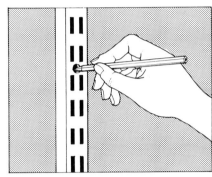

1 Place an end upright in the correct position (holding it in place with masking tape if necessary — but first check it will not damage your paintwork or wallpaper) and mark the topmost screw hole by poking a pencil in the screw hole and making a mark on the wall.

2 Wrap masking tape around the drill bit to mark the depth the screw holes need to be, move the upright out of the way, then drill a hole in the marked position for the top fixing, and loosely fix the upright in place, using just the top hole and following the manufacturer's instructions.

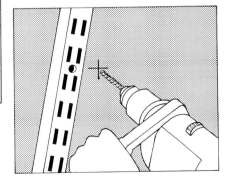

3 Allow the upright to swing freely and act

as its own plumb line, and mark every other screw hole on the wall. Swing the upright out of the way (hold it with masking tape if necessary) and drill holes where you have marked, making sure you drill accurately. Swing the upright back in position and insert the fixings.

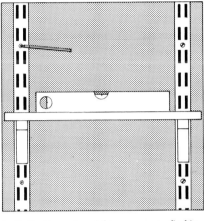

4 To fix the next upright, measure to find its position, then check each one is level by placing a spirit level on a shelf laid across a bracket fitted at the same point on each upright.

5 Adjust the position until the uprights are exactly level, then repeat steps 1, 2 and 3 until you have finished all the uprights.

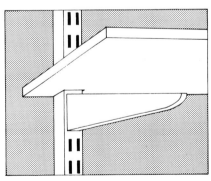

6 For extra security, cut square notches out of the back of each shelf to fit round the uprights, and always screw the shelves to the brackets. Different makes of adjustable shelving systems have different ways of fixing shelves securely. Some simply screw in, others use clips which screw under the shelves and locate into the supports.

Left Opposite: Stencilling in pretty colours gives a co-ordinated look to the corner of this nursery and adds a special touch to the cot. The stencil is from a range of ready-cut designs and using such a stencil is a good way to gain confidence if you do not feel ready yet to produce your own designs.

Safety note: If you stencil on the inside of a cot as here, make sure the paint you use and the surface you are working on are compatible. It is very important that paint does not flake off as a baby could swallow it.

Above: An adjustable shelving system makes most sense for a nursery as it can cope with change better than any other type. This, of course, is very important where growing children are involved. Opt for a sturdy design which will allow for the future storage of books, hi-fi equipment and so on. If necessary you can swop some of the

shelves and brackets for deeper ones at a later date.

For safety's sake always screw the shelves to the brackets so that children cannot pull them down on to themselves. The shelves are made from medium density fibreboard (MDF) which is strong and easy to paint. It has been painted with eggshell paint to match the wall. Simple stencilling has been carried out in primrose yellow to tone with the curtains.

Cheap, colourful, stacking plastic crates or plastic-coated wire baskets are also useful for storing toys. These crates can be kept on low, deep shelves or on the floor to encourage your child to put things away after use. This is important because a small child will probably not be able to open drawers or cupboard doors, but even a toddler can learn to put things in a crate and tidy up after himself. Castors are available to fit on some types of crate.

The exception to the advice not to buy child-sized furniture for the nursery is that a child can derive a lot of pleasure and use from a child-sized table and chair (or chairs), and these are available in very inexpensive plastic versions. To make sure the furniture is a suitable size for your child, check that, when seated, his feet can touch the floor and that the table top is at elbow height. An even cheaper alternative is to cut down the legs of a small, old table to child level, and cover blocks of foam with fabric to use as seats.

Covering a block of foam to make a seat

Foam blocks make very handy and inexpensive seating, and can be easily covered with fabric. Smaller blocks make wonderfully squashy play bricks.

You will need

A block of combusion modified foam large enough for your child to sit on
Fabric for covering
Thread

1 Measure up each of the sides of the foam block. Draw a pattern for the top/bottom and sides, adding 1.5 cm (⅝ in) all round for seams. Cut out the pieces. At this stage you may like to appliqué, embroider or paint (using fabric paints) designs on the different surfaces. Alternatively you can choose a patterned fabric, or a mixture of plain, bright colours for the different sides.
2 Lay out the side pieces to form a line, making sure they are in the correct order and each piece is the correct way round.

3 Machine the pieces together to form a strip, right sides facing and taking 1.5 cm (⅝ in) seam allowance, but only sew as far as the corner of the seam allowance each time, do not sew right up to the edge. Press the seams open then press under the 1.5 cm (⅝ in) seam allowance at either end.

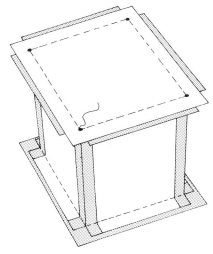

4 Pin the sides to the top and bottom as shown, opening out the seams at the corners. Tack then machine in place, pivoting the needle at each corner.
5 Slip the foam block into the cover and through the slot. Oversew the edges together.

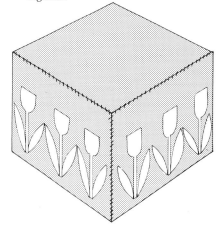

Making a simple chair cover
You will need

An old upholstered dining chair, with the legs cut down if necessary
Fabric for covering
Piping cord

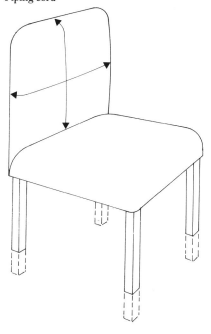

1 Measure the height of the back of the chair from the seat, and measure the width of the chair back. Cut two pieces of fabric about 5 cm (2 in) bigger all round than this measurement.

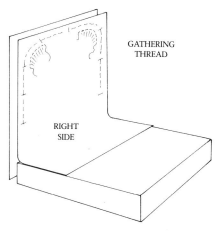

GATHERING THREAD

RIGHT SIDE

2 Pin them together over the back of the chair, right sides outwards. You may

need to run a gathering thread around the top corners to get a good fit.

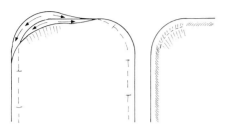

3 Trim the seam allowance to 1.5 cm (⅝ in) all round. Open up the seam allowance and rub chalk along it to mark the seam line. Remove the cover and unpin the seam.

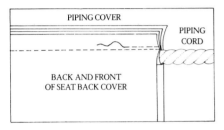

PIPING COVER

PIPING CORD

BACK AND FRONT OF SEAT BACK COVER

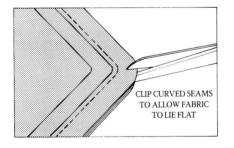

CLIP CURVED SEAMS TO ALLOW FABRIC TO LIE FLAT

4 Prepare enough covered piping (see below) to go along the seam line. Pin the front and back together, right sides together, sandwich the piping between the two, following the chalk-marked seam allowance. Tack through all thicknesses, try on the chair back to check all is well, then machine along the seam line.

5 Cut a piece of fabric about 5 cm (2 in) bigger all round than the chair seat. Put the back cover on the back of the chair, right side out. Pin the seat fabric in place, right side up. Pin the seam where

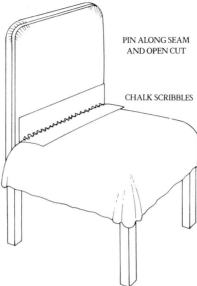

PIN ALONG SEAM AND OPEN CUT

CHALK SCRIBBLES

the seat meets the back, matching up any pattern if necessary. Open out the pinned seam and chalk along the line.

6 Remove all pins then trim the seam allowance on both pieces to 1.5 cm

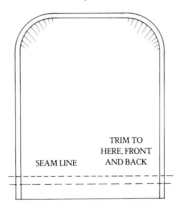

TRIM TO HERE, FRONT AND BACK

SEAM LINE

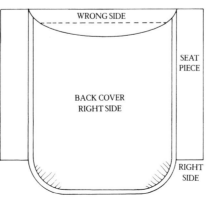

WRONG SIDE

SEAT PIECE

BACK COVER RIGHT SIDE

RIGHT SIDE

(⅜ in), trimming the back of the back cover to match the front. Repin the back cover to the seat, right sides together, and sew along the seam line.

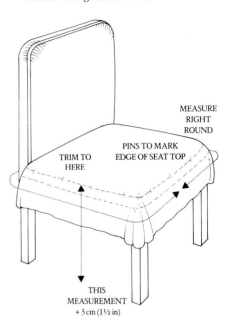

MEASURE RIGHT ROUND

PINS TO MARK EDGE OF SEAT TOP

TRIM TO HERE

THIS MEASUREMENT + 3 cm (1½ in)

7 Put the cover back on the chair and establish where the edges of the seat is going to be. Mark this with a row of pins, then measure from the pins to the floor. Measure all round the seat (passing the tape measure round behind the back). Cut a piece of fabric 1½ times the measurement round the seat, with a depth that is the measurement from the seat to the floor plus 3 cm (1 ¼in).

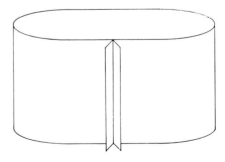

8 Sew the short ends of the fabric together, right sides facing, to form a loop of fabric. Press the seam open.
Continued on page 84

Above: Furniture systems with matching components often offer a stylish solution to nursery storage problems. This made-to-measure range, although obviously designed with babies very much in mind, also offers generously proportioned storage which will last a child into adulthood.

The changing area is well-planned with everything to hand — a very important consideration as you should not leave your baby for a second while he is on a raised changing surface.

Right: The only piece of furniture you really need to buy specially for a baby's room is a cot. The rest can, if necessary, be improvised. Here a second-hand wardrobe has been stripped down to the bare wood and refinished with non-toxic varnish. The hanging rail has been lowered, and shelves have been fitted above it. The rail can be returned to its proper position and the shelves removed once the child grows enough to need taller hanging space.

The upholstered chair is for the parents to sit in when feeding the baby, and the low chest of drawers doubles as a changing unit. The different pieces work well together even though they are different styles because they are all natural wood.

Safety note: If you are thinking of using a second-hand cot, make very sure that it conforms to the latest safety regulations, or you could be putting your child at risk.

SAME AS MEASUREMENT ROUND SEAT

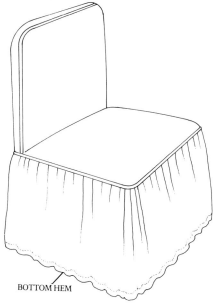

BOTTOM HEM

9 Run two parallel gathering threads around the top edge of the fabric and arrange the gathers evenly.

10 Prepare enough covered piping to run around the edge of the seat and across the back.

SEAT COVER

SKIRT -WRONG SIDE

BACK COVER

11 Right sides together, pin the gathers to the edge of the seat cover and across the back, sandwiching the piping in as you go.

12 Pin, then tack the seam. Machine through all thicknesses.

13 Turn up the bottom hem 5 mm (¼ in), then 1 cm (⅜ in) and machine or hand sew in place.

Making covered piping

Piping gives a neat finish to a seam, as well as protecting it from wear. To work out the amount of piping cord you need, measure the length of the seam lines that need piping, add an extra 5 cm (2 in) for each join and a little extra for shrinkage. Piping cord tends to shrink so wash and dry it before use to ensure it is thoroughly shrunk. Be careful not to pull the binding out of shape when you are making it or it will lose its stretchiness and ability to curve neatly round corners.

Make sufficient bias binding to cover your piping. For this you can use the same fabric as the item to be piped, or you can choose a contrasting fabric. To measure the width of binding you need, cut a strip of fabric and wrap it around the cord as shown. Pin the fabric close to the piping and to this measurement add the seam allowance 1.5 cm

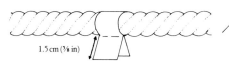

1.5 cm (⅜ in)

(⅜ in). Cut the fabric at this point, open it out flat and measure it to discover the width of binding you need.

Method 1

1 You can make small quantities of bias binding by taking a rectangle of fabric and folding the selvedge across at right angles, so it lies along the crosswise grain of the fabric.

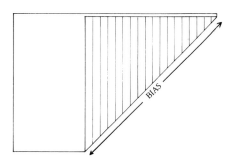

BIAS

2 Press the fabric to form a crease and draw lines parallel to it, each your calculated distance apart.

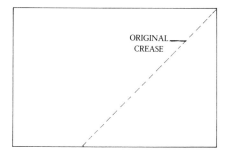

ORIGINAL CREASE

3 To join strips together you must join the fabric at an angle. Place the fabric right sides together as shown, machine along the seam line, taking a 6 mm (½ in) seam allowance.

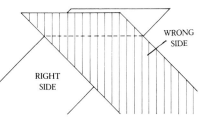

WRONG SIDE

RIGHT SIDE

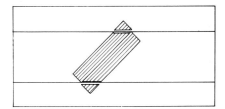

4   Press the seam open and trim off the corners.

Method 2

1   To make larger quantities of bias binding cut a rectangle of fabric twice as long as it is wide. With the wrong side of the fabric facing you and looking at the fabric longways on, fold the top right hand corner down towards you so that what was the top edge now lies along the left side.

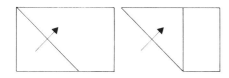

2   Press the fabric along this line, then cut along the fold.

3   Sew this triangle on to the bottom of the fabric, right sides facing, taking a 6 mm (½ in) seam allowance. Press the seam open.

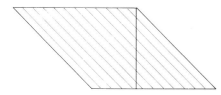

4   Draw parallel lines on the wrong side of the fabric, each one the width you want

your binding to be (as with the previous method), starting at the top diagonal cut edge.

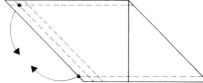

5   Draw a 6 mm (½ in) seam line down either long side, and mark two points along the line as shown.
6   Working from the wrong side, put a pin through one point and bring it across to the other.
7   Keeping these points exactly together, pin the edges together along the seam line, forming a tube with a diagonal seam, and making sure that the diagonal lines link up exactly.

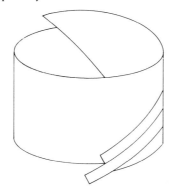

8   Tack along the seam allowance, then machine along it.

9   Starting at the top, cut along the drawn lines to form a continuous spiral of bias binding.

Covering the cord

1   Fold the bias strip around the cord with the right side of the fabric outwards and the raw edges level.

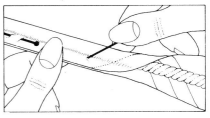

2   Pin, then stitch close to the cord using a zipper foot.

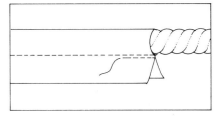

Joining covered piping

If a continuous seam is piped, the piping will have to be joined.
1   Cut the piping 12 cm (4¾ in) longer than the seam and unpick the stitching for a few centimetres (inches).

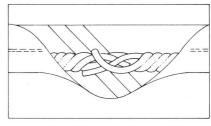

2   Join the binding with a diagonal seam.
3   Trim the cord so it overlaps slightly. Unravel the strands a little and cut each one to a different length, then twist them together and wrap cotton thread around to hold them in place.

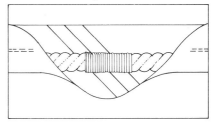

Left: Child-sized tables and chairs may be outgrown fairly quickly but they give a lot of pleasure and scope for imaginative play. And if you choose inexpensive versions, such as these, you will not mind too much when they have to be swopped for something bigger. Being plastic they are light, durable and easy to clean should anything get spilt on them.

Safety note: Do not leave children alone at a table with desk lamp until they are old enough to respect electricity.

Above: A traditional toy box with a lid makes a very attractive home for a child's most treasured possessions. This one boasts a beautiful hand-stencilled design, sturdy construction and an adjustable lid-stay to help protect tiny fingers.

Making a shaped headboard for a child's bed

This headboard is in a sheep design, and is intended for a 100 cm (40 in) wide bed, but you could make one to any size and to any design.

You will need

A piece of 12 mm (½ in) medium density fibreboard (MDF)
Two strips of 7.5 × 2.5 cm (3 × 1 in) softwood each 1 m (1 yd) long
Electric jigsaw
White eggshell paint
Artist's acrylics or PVA paint

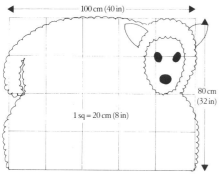

1 Lightly chalk 20 cm (8 in) squares on the MDF and transfer the design from the diagram.
2 Cut out the shape using an electric jigsaw.
3 Notch the ends of the softwood strips so they fit over the screws at the back of the divan.
4 Position the strips on the back of the

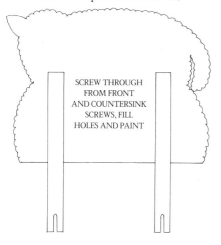

headboard so that when the notches are resting on the screws the headboard will be in the right position. Screw them in place from the front of the headboard, countersinking the screw heads.

5 Fill the screw holes with filler and allow to dry. Then give the headboard a coat of primer. Give it two coats of white eggshell, allowing each to dry, then paint in the details with artist's acrylics or PVA paint.

RESTORING FURNITURE

Preparing all wood surfaces

You will need

Hot-air paint stripper (see below)
Sugar soap (see below)
Hot soapy water and scrubbing brush (see below)
Liquid sander
Wet and dry paper
Knotting (shellac)

1 If you know the piece of furniture has previously been painted with non-toxic paint which is in good condition, you can paint straight over it (although you will get better results if you strip the paint off completely). Wash the piece down with sugar soap to remove dirt and grime. Rinse well. Then rub it down with wet and dry paper or liquid sander to give a key.
2 If the surface has a wax coating, remove this using wax cleaner. Otherwise stand the piece on plenty of newspapers and strip off all old paint and varnish using a chemical or hot-air stripper. Chemical strippers give off fumes, so pregnant women are not recommended to use them. However, if you wish to use chemical strippers, be sure to follow the instructions carefully.
3 Scrub the stripped furniture down with hot soapy water and allow to dry (this may take several days), then rub over with wet and dry paper, along the grain of the wood.
4 Fill any holes with wood filler to just above the surface and, when dry, rub down with wet and dry paper wrapped

around a sanding block or handy-sized block of wood. If you intend varnishing the furniture use wood filler coloured to match the wood.
5 If you want to varnish the furniture and then paint or stencil on it use a fairly matt varnish. If you are going to paint the furniture, treat any knots with knotting.
6 If you are going to paint the furniture, bare wood will need a coat of primer. If you are intending using liquid gloss you will also need an undercoat (see Choosing and using paints, Chapter 2), although if you intend painting, stencilling or carrying out paint effects on the piece, you will need to use eggshell (use two coats, rubbing down lightly between coats with wet and dry paper).

Painting and decorating furniture

Furniture for a child's room can look really special if decorated with stencilling, paint effects or painting, or a mixture of two or three of these. Paint effects give a textured background that can make a good surface on which to stencil or paint, or which can look very attractive in its own right and is certainly more interesting than plain paint.

Putting new handles on furniture can make all the difference to is appearance, and you may even be able to make a new piece of budget furniture look more classy simply by buying new handles for it. Alternatively you can make novelty handles for furniture. When the child outgrows them you can replace them with something more sophisticated.

Making novelty handles for furniture

You will need

Wood or board 1–2 cm (⅜–¾ in) thick for the handles

Strips of 1.5–2 cm (⅝–¾ in) softwood for the backs of the handles

Woodworking adhesive

Screws

1 Cut out the shape and glue a piece of softwood on the back as a support.

2 Using a countersink screw long enough to hold the handle on the front of the drawer without the screw coming out the other side, drill a hole through the centre of the handle and screw the handle to the furniture, countersinking the screw head.

3 Fill the screw hole with filler and allow to dry, sand the filler flat, then prime the handle and allow to dry.

4 Paint the handle using eggshell and/or acrylic paint.

LIQUORICE ALLSORTS CHEST OF DRAWERS

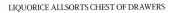
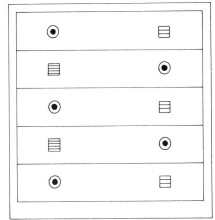

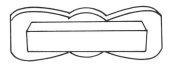
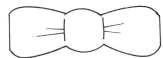

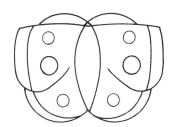

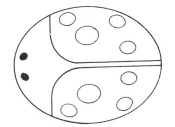

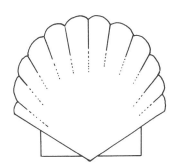
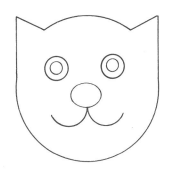

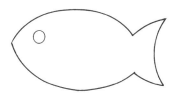

Left: Decorated throughout with a sheep theme, this child's room demonstrates how effective a range of co-ordinating linens, wallcoverings and fabrics can be. The motif has also been stencilled on the chest of drawers and a matching sheep-shaped bed-head has been constructed from painted plywood.

Above: Older children may like to provide designs for their own and younger children's furniture and may even like to help with the decorating themselves (but be sure to supervise them closely). Paint the furniture first with two coats of eggshell base coat and paint the designs freehand using artist's acrylics (make sure the colours you choose are non-toxic), nursery enamels, eggshell paint or PVA paints. The designs can also be copied on to bedlinen by carrying out designs on white sheeting using fabric paints and cutting out the designs and appliquéing them on to duvet covers and pillows.

Left: This beautiful chest of drawers has been dragged with pink paint, then has been hand-painted with ribbons and posies of flowers. The changing box on the top has deep sides to prevent a baby rolling off and can be used later to store toys under the bed.

PAINT EFFECTS FOR FURNITURE

Using paint treatments on the simplest pieces of furniture can subtly transform them from being dull and past their best to works of art. Do not forget that you can mix two or more paint effects on one piece of furniture — sponging, for example, looks good in the centres of door panels, while dragging looks better (and is easier to do) round the edges.

Paint effects on furniture must be done on an eggshell basecoat. Experts then carry out the effect on top of this using a scumble glaze, which involves making a mixture of transparent oil glaze, white spirit and paint. The advantage of this is that it stays wet long enough for you to carry out the effect. However, it is perfectly possible just to use eggshell glaze (eggshell thinned with a little white spirit) for most effects. You will need to experiment on scrap material to ensure you have the right consistency. If you find it dries too quickly for you to complete the effect, you can add a teaspoon (5 ml) of boiled linseed oil (available from art shops and specialist paint stores) to about 500 ml (¾ pt) of glaze.

Combing

Combing produces fine, parallel lines on furniture and is most suited to smaller pieces with flat surfaces. Choose fairly closely related colours for a subtle effect.

You will need

Eggshell paint for the base coat
Brush to apply it
Eggshell glaze for combing (see above)
Paintbrush for applying the top coat
Metal or rubber graining comb (from specialist paint shops) or substitute such as tile adhesive spreader

1 Prepare the furniture and apply the base colour in eggshell, as described above. Allow to dry.
2 Working on small areas at a time, paint on the eggshell glaze. Stipple over the painted surface with the bristles of the

brush to obliterate the brush strokes.
3 While the paint is still wet, pull the comb through it, using one continuous stroke from top to bottom. Wipe off any glaze on the comb using a rag or paper towel.

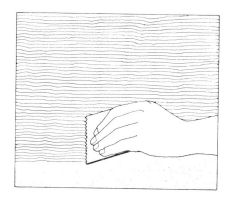

4 Repeat this procedure until you have covered the surface, then leave to dry.
5 Different effects can be achieved by criss-crossing the strokes to form a basket weave pattern, or by drawing the comb down in wavy lines or zig-zags.

Dragging

Dragging produces a softer, more subtle effect than combing. To drag properly you need a special brush called a 'dragger'. However, these brushes are expensive and it is possible to create a fair approximation using an ordinary household paintbrush or paperhanging brush.

You will need

Base coat of eggshell
Brush to apply base coat
Eggshell glaze for dragging
Paint kettle or similar container to mix the glaze in
A wide brush to apply the glaze
A special dragging brush, wide paintbrush, about 12 cm (5 in) or paperhanging brush to drag through the glaze.

1 Paint the base coat in eggshell and allow to dry. Mix up the glaze (choose a fairly strong colour for the glaze as the final effect will look considerably lighter) and paint it on in small sections.
2 Draw the dragging brush down through the glaze with a continuous, light, steady movement, leaving faint stripes in the glaze. Wipe your brush on a rag every time you complete a line. Continue until you reach the edge of the band, then paint another band and repeat the process.

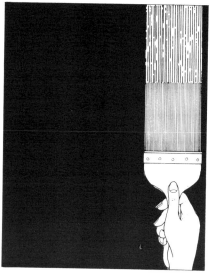

If you do wish to try your hand at paint effects on furniture the professional way using a scumble glaze, you will need to mix one up yourself. Take a small amount of ready-mixed transparent oil glaze (see address list for suppliers) and stir appropriately coloured artist's oil paint into it until it is a darker version of the colour you want — and smooth, with no lumps. Pour this mixture into a paint kettle containing the amount of oil glaze you think you will need to complete the job. Then add one part thinner (white spirit, which dries quickly, or turpentine which dries slowly) to six parts glaze. Use as described above.

PAINTING ON FURNITURE

Freehand work on furniture can look very charming, and any mistakes or wobbly bits add to the charm. For inspiration look at books on folk art furniture and children's paintings. You can use eggshell, gloss paint, special nursery enamels, PVA paints and artist's acrylics (make sure that the colours you buy are non-toxic). See also the section on mural painting in Chapter 2 for information on choosing and using these types of paints, and to see which types of brushes are most appropriate.

Positioning painted designs

1 If you are decorating drawers or doors you may need to remove knobs or handles. Take into account the shape and types of surfaces that the piece of furniture has, and work out a design which complements and emphasizes them. The design should also be in proportion to the size of the piece of furniture — a large motif would look overwhelming on a small piece of furniture, while a small motif on a big piece will look tiny and lost.

2 For best results, sketch out your ideas first on paper, actual size. Designs do not have to be entirely figurative or accurate. Blobs and squiggles can look very exciting, and remember you can combine paint effects with the designs for extra interest.

3 Cut out the sketches of the motifs and position them on the piece of furniture to make sure they are the correct size and scale. Make sure you centre motifs accurately: measure carefully to find the right position, do not use guesswork.

4 When you have decided on your design, draw it on to the piece of furniture with white chalk.

5 Start off by painting in the blocks of main colour, then paint details over the top. Use old tins, plates and yoghurt pots for mixing up colours. Use masking tape as a guide for painting straight lines.

Stencilling on to furniture

Stencilling is a simple way to bring colour, pattern and a personal touch to furniture. The basic principles of stencilling have been covered in chapter 2. Paint the furniture first with two coats of background colour using eggshell and allow to dry. For positioning stencilled motifs, see Positioning painted designs above.

OTHER EQUIPMENT YOU MAY NEED FOR THE NURSERY

Baby baths

These are not essential but are very useful. Instead you can use a large washing-up bowl. Baby baths are now often ergonomically designed so that the baby's back is supported, a textured surface helps prevent the baby slipping, and you only need the minimum amount of water, making easy work of filling, carrying and emptying the bath. Some nappy-changing units contain a baby bath (see below).

The safest place to use a bath is on the floor (put some towels down first) or on a sturdy, wipe-clean table. Some baths come with stands, but check these are sturdy enough, and do not use a stand with any bath other than the one it is intended for. Stands sometimes double as a useful carry-cot holder or crib stand, so these are worth considering. Do not use a baby bath on a stand once your child can stand up on his own, and move the child to the big bath when he is between about three and six months old.

Changing units

These provide somewhere to change your baby and usually include storage space for nappies and toiletries. Some include a bath as well. You can, of course, place a changing mat on top of a chest of drawers or worktop instead, in which case you can arrange for lots of storage space to be near at hand and you can provide a mobile to occupy your baby or you can change your baby on a protective mat on the floor. Wherever you decide, make sure the area is warm and free from draughts.

Safety note: Never leave your baby alone on a raised surface, even for a moment.

Playpens

These are not an essential item, so consider whether you are going to really need one. Playpens take up space and some babies simply do not like them, so try your child out first before parting with any money. However, you cannot be sure that everything in your house is safe, so it can be a useful way of making sure that your child does not come to harm while you are busy.

Choose from a wooden design or a mesh version with a padded edge. Both should have a built-in floor so that the child cannot push the playpen across the room.

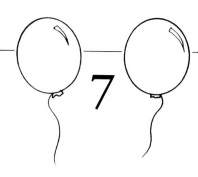

7

BEDDING AND BEDLINEN

You will need quite a lot of bedding for your child in the first few years, and choosing the right type, and in sufficient quantities, will make life a lot easier for you. Safety is also an important consideration, so follow recommendations carefully.

Bedding, being mostly flat shapes, is simple to make and can represent quite a saving, especially if you recycle old sheets of your own. You can buy sheeting by the metre (yard): probably the most suitable fabric is cotton polyester because it combines the absorbency of cotton with the easy-care qualities of polyester. It usually comes in two widths — 175 cm (68¾ in) and 230 cm (90½ in) — so bear this in mind as, depending on what you are making, one width may work out more economical than another. If you buy fabric by the metre (yard) for making bed linen, only buy proper sheeting as any other fabric will be too coarse for a small child's delicate skin.

For a baby's first bed — a Moses basket or carry-cot — you will need at least six sheets, at least two blankets and at least one top cover. You must not use a pillow for a child under a year old (even so-called 'safety pillows'), as this could cause suffocation, and once the child is old enough, use a safety cot pillow. Only use a safety mattress for a baby, (see Chapter 6 for information on choosing cots and mattresses) which has a waterproof covering stopping short of the vented head

end. Blankets for babies should be machine washable, and preferably cellular. Check that they are closely woven, with no loose bits that a baby could catch his fingers in, and that there are no fraying parts that he could chew and choke on. Although he will only be in a Moses basket or carry-cot for a maximum of six months, you will also be able to make use of this bedding in the pram.

Once he moves up to a cot he will need at least three pairs of sheets plus two blankets or a duvet with at least two covers. You may prefer to use fitted terry bottom sheets which are easy to fit, absorbent and more comfy for the baby. If you opt for a duvet, make sure it is machine washable. There has been a suggestion that, like pillows, duvets are not suitable for children under a year old as they could cause suffocation. However, duvets are sold as being suitable for small babies so you must decide for yourself on this. Always use a safety mattress in a cot, and remember that only one end has air vents, so do not put the child up the other end without turning the mattress round.

A cot is a wonderful size for making decorative quilts and bedding, as not so much work or materials are involved as for a full-size bed. You can edge top sheets with pretty fabric to blend in with the room scheme, or embroider them, if you are using blankets, and you can also make patchwork or appliqué quilts or duvet covers. Once the child has

outgrown his cot, a decorative quilt can always be displayed on the wall as a hanging. The loveliest idea for a cot quilt is the traditional American album quilt, for which friends and relatives each contribute a square. Instructions are given later in this chapter.

When your child graduates to a proper bed he will need two pairs of top and bottom sheets and at least two washable blankets, or a minimum of two bottom sheets plus a washable duvet and two covers. He will also need a pillow and at least two pillowcases.

Cot bumpers

A cot bumper protects a baby from draughts and from knocking his head against the sides of the cot. Use one at either end of the cot for extra comfort if you like. Make sure the ties are securely fastened at all times and do not use with a child once he is old enough to stand or he may step on the bumper to help him climb out of the cot. Cot bumpers should tie only at the top, not the lower edge near the mattress, and ties must not be more than 30 cm (12 in) long.

You will need

Cotton or cotton polyester fabric
Polyester wadding
6 cm (2⅜ in) bias binding
Ribbon for ties

1 Cut the pieces of fabric 60 cm (24 in) wide by 35 cm (14 in) deep (these will be the side pieces), and two pieces of fabric the inside width of the cot plus 3 cm (1⅛ in), by 35 cm (14 in) deep (these will be the end pieces). Cut a piece of wadding the inside width of the cot plus 107 cm (42¾ in) long, by 35 cm (14 in) wide.

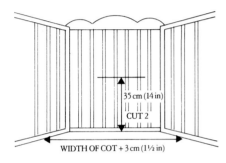

2 Join two end pieces to either side of the centre pieces, right sides together and with 1.5 cm (⅝ in) seams, to form two long strips of fabric.

3 Press seams open, and make a sandwich of the fabric, the wadding and the lining, with the right sides of the fabric facing outwards. Tack all round the raw edges.

4 Machine-quilt along the two seam lines.

5 Mark vertical lines every 10 cm (4 in), using tailor's chalk (make sure it will rub off) or a vanishing marker. Machine-quilt along these lines. This is to help the bumper stand up straight.

6 Bind round the edges with bias binding. See pages 49–50 and 85 for instructions on binding edges and bias binding.

7 Sew ribbons to the back of the bumper near the top (not at the bottom, where the child could reach them), to hold in place on the cot bars. Keep ribbons as short as possible.

To make a flat sheet for a cot or single bed

To make a flat sheet for a standard cot 118 × 56 cm (46½ × 22 in) deep or for a standard single bed 190 by 90 cm

You will need

Cotton polyester sheeting
Thread to match

1 For the cot sheet cut a piece of fabric 170 × 105 cm (67 × 42 in). For the single

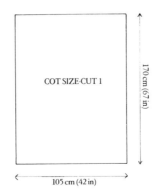

bed sheet cut a piece of fabric 265 by 180 cm (104¼ × 70¾ in).

2 Turn both side edges under 5 mm (¼ in) towards the wrong side and press. then turn under another 1 cm (⅜ in) on each side, press, pin and machine-stitch.

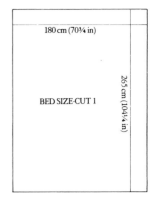

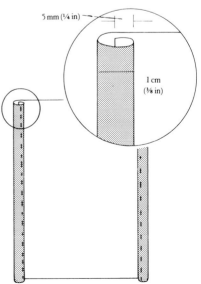

3 At the top end turn 1 cm (⅜ in) towards the wrong side and press, then turn under another 5 cm (2 in), press, pin and machine-stitch. You can, if you like, tack this seam, then sew it from the right side with coloured zig-zag stitches or machine or hand embroidery.

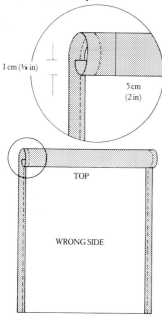

4 Turn the bottom hem under 5 mm (¼ in) towards the wrong side and press, turn under a further 3 cm (1⅛ in), press, pin and machine stitch.

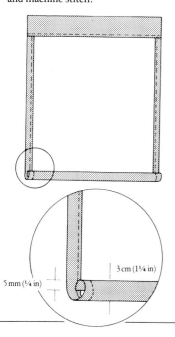

Making a pillowcase for a cot or single bed
You will need

Cotton or cotton polyester sheeeting
for a cot pillow 57 × 35 cm (22¾ × 14 in), you will need one piece 144 × 40.5 cm (57⅛ × 16¼ in);
for a bed pillow 74 × 48 cm (29⅝ × 19¼ in) you will need one piece 178 × 53.5 cm (71¼ × 21⅜ in)

1 Cut fabric to size, depending on the size of pillow you are using.

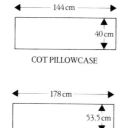

2 Make a line of tacking 20 cm (8 in) from one end, then make a narrow double hem at this end. Turn under 5 cm (¼ in) to the wrong side then another 5 cm (¼ in), press and machine-stitch.

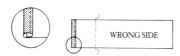

3 Turn the other end under 1.5 cm (⅝ in) to the wrong side, press, then turn under another 6 cm (2½ in), press and stitch in place. If you wish to do hand or machine embroidery along this seam, do so at this stage.

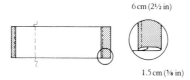

4 Lay the piece of fabric on a flat surface, right side upwards, with the narrow hem

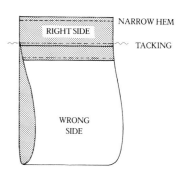

at the top and fold the wide hem up to meet the tacking line.

5 Fold down the narrow hemmed piece of fabric, along the tacking line, to cover the wide hem. Tack through all thicknesses down both sides and machine, taking a 1.5 cm (⅝ in) seam. Remove all tacking, turn to the right side and press.

Making a duvet cover for a cot or single bed

Making a duvet cover yourself not only works out cheaper than buying one ready-made, but you can choose your fabric and decorate it in any way you please. Ready-made covers are usually patterned, or are a different colour on either side and the combination may not blend in with your colour scheme. Also, a ready-made cover is difficult to work with if you want to do machine embroidery on it, or print on it with fabric paints, for example. If you are intending doing the latter, choose cotton fabric as the dye takes better on pure natural fibre.

You will need

Cotton or cotton polyester sheeting
for a cot duvet 120×100 cm (48×40 in), you will need two pieces 125×103 cm ($50 \times 41\frac{1}{4}$ in);
for a single bed duvet 200×135 cm (80×54 in), you will need two pieces 205×138 cm ($82 \times 55\frac{1}{4}$ in)
Fastening: 1 cm ($\frac{3}{8}$ in) wide cotton tape in colour to match cover — 150 cm (60 in) for cot cover and 240 cm (96 in) for bed cover; or snap fastener tape, up to 2 cm ($\frac{3}{4}$ in) wide — 60 cm (24 in) for the cot cover or 90 cm (36 in) for the bed cover; or 2 cm ($\frac{3}{4}$ in) Velcro dots to match the fabric — six for the cot cover or nine for the bed cover

1   Cut fabric to size, depending on the cover you are making. If your duvet is a

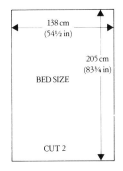

different size from the measurements given, reduce or enlarge the two pieces of fabric by this amount, e.g. if your duvet is 10 cm (4 in) longer, add 10 cm (4 in) to the length of each piece of fabric; if it is 10 cm (4 in) narrower, reduce the width of each piece of fabric by 10 cm (4 in). If you want to decorate the cover in any way do it at this stage.

2   If you are using tape fastenings, lay the pieces of fabric bottom end to bottom

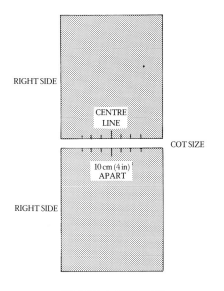

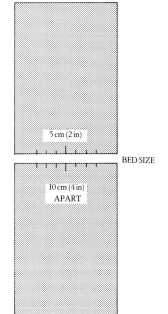

end, right side up, and find the centre point of the bottom edge of each piece. Mark this point close to the edge of the fabric using a pencil, tailor's chalk or vanishing cloth marker. For the quilt, make two extra marks, each 10 cm (4 in) apart, on either side of the centre line, making five in all. For the bed quilt, make a mark 5 cm (2 in) either side of the centre line, then a further three marks, each 10 cm (4 in) apart, on both sides, making eight in all (ignore the centre line marking for the bed cover). Transfer the markings across to the other piece of fabric, making sure the marks line up exactly with each other.

3   Cut ten pieces of tape 15 cm (6 in) long for the cot quilt and sixteen pieces 15 cm (6 in) long for the bed quilt. Turn one end of each piece of tape under 5 mm ($\frac{1}{4}$ in) and zig-zag stitch, straight machine-stitch or hand-sew in place.

4   Place one tape on each mark (not on the centre mark of the bed size), right sides together and raw edges level at the bottom. Tack each tape in place 1 cm ($\frac{3}{8}$ in) from the bottom edge, and again 10 cm (4 in) from the bottom edge.

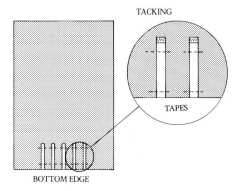

5   Whichever method of fastening you are using, turn the bottom edge of each piece of fabric under 1 cm (⅜ in) to the wrong side, tack, machine and press.

WRONG SIDE

(VELCRO OR SNAP FASTENING)

1 cm (⅜ in)

WRONG SIDE

(TAPE FASTENING)

ENDS OF TAPES

6   If you are using Velcro dots or snap fastener tape, turn the fabric pieces to the right side, draw two tailor's chalk or vanishing marker lines, one 12 mm (½ in) and one 2.5 cm (1 in) from, and parallel to, the bottom edge.

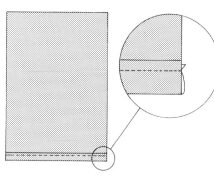

7   If you are using Velcro dots, make marks along the 12 mm (½ in) line, using the method for the tapes in step 2, and sew (following manufacturer's instructions) one dot per mark on the line, putting all the hooked dots on one piece of fabric and all the looped dots on the other.

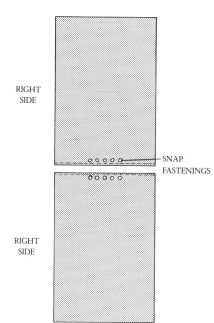

RIGHT SIDE

SNAP FASTENINGS

RIGHT SIDE

8   If you are using snap fastener tape, mark the centre of the 12 mm (½ in) lines, and place the centre of the tapes on these lines. Check that the press studs line up with each other on the two pieces of fabric. Tack the tape in place, making sure the centre, lengthways, of the tape lies along the 12 mm (½ in) line. Machine in place along both edges of tape.

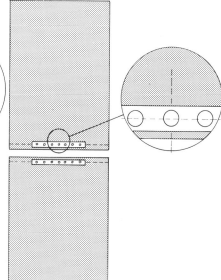

9   Place the two pieces of fabric right sides together and bottom seams together. Taking a 2.5 cm (1 in) seam allowance, sew in from each end 21.5 cm (8⅝ in) for the cot quilt or 24 cm (9⅝ in) for the bed quilt along the hemmed bottom edge.

WRONG SIDE

24 cm (9¼ in)

2.5 cm (1 in)

10   Taking a 1.5 cm (⅝ in) seam allowance, sew around the other three sides.

WRONG SIDE

11   Trim corners slightly (do not cut too near stitching) and turn right sides out. Remove any tacking and press.

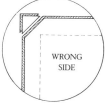

WRONG SIDE

Note: when in use, always make sure the end of the cover with the fastenings is at the bottom end of the cot or bed.

This enchanting pillowcase and duvet cover provide scope for all sorts of imaginative games, as well as offering ideas for murals, stencils and mobiles. The jolly colours can be matched to other plain and patterned fabrics, forming the basis of a complete room scheme.

Making a patchwork duvet cover

This patchwork duvet cover looks as though it requires a lot of skill, yet in fact it is very simple to make. It is also a good way of making a more expensive nursery print go further, by spacing it out with plain fabrics, or you could decorate some of the squares yourself, perhaps with fabric printing or embroidery, before assembling it. You could also make pillowcases to match, plus the quilted rug, on page 48, for a completely co-ordinated look. Make sure that the fabrics you use for this cover are all sheeting weight. If they vary it means the cover will not wear so well, plus heavier fabric would be un-comfortable next to a child's skin. If you have chosen two striped fabrics for fabrics B and C, as in the photograph, you can give greater variety by using one horizontally and the other vertically. But you will need to plan the layout carefully first, to make sure that you cut the rectangles the right way round.

You will need
For a cot quilt cover to fit a duvet
120 × 100 cm (48 × 40 in):
Cotton or cotton polyester sheeting
Fabric A — 13 × 23 cm (9¼ in) squares, plus
2 × 23 × 25 cm (9¼ × 10 in) rectangles
Fabric B — 6 × 23 cm (9¼ in) squares, plus
1 × 23 × 25 cm (9¼ × 10 in) rectangle
Fabric C — 6 × 23 cm (9¼ in) squares, plus
2 × 23 × 25 cm (9¼ × 10 in) rectangles
Fabric for the back of the quilt —
125 × 103 cm (50 × 41¼ in)
Fastening: 150 cm (60 in) of 1 cm (⅜ in) wide cotton tape in a colour to co-ordinate with cover; or 60 cm (24 in) of snap fastener tape, up to 2 cm (¾ in) wide; or six 2 cm (¾ in) Velcro dots in a colour to co-ordinate with the fabric.

For a single bed quilt cover to fit a duvet
200 × 135 cm (80 × 54 in):
Cotton or cotton polyester sheeting
Fabric A — 32 × 22.2 × 23 cm (8¾ × 9¼ in) rectangles , plus 3 × 22.2 × 25 cm (8¾ × 10 in) rectangles
Fabric B — 16 × 22.2 × 23 cm (8¾ × 9¼ in) rectangles , plus 2 × 22.2 × 25 cm

(8¾ × 10 in) rectangles
Fabric C — 15 × 22.2 × 23 cm (8¾ × 9¼ in) rectangles, plus 2 × 22.2 × 25 cm (8¾ × 10 in) rectangles
Fabric for the back of the quilt —
205 × 138 cm (82 × 55¼ in)
Fastening: 240 cm (96 in) of 1 cm (⅜ in) wide cotton tape in a colour to co-ordinate with cover; or 90 cm (36 in) of snap fastener tape, up to 2 cm (¾ in) wide; or nine 2 cm (¾ in) Velcro dots in a colour to co-ordinate with the fabric.

1 Cut out the squares and lay them out, face upward, in the order shown. The longer rectangles make up the bottom row.

23 cm (9 in)

A	B	A	C	A
C	A	B	A	C
A	C	A	B	A
B	A	C	A	B
A	B	A	C	A
C	A	B	A	C

25 cm (10 in)

COT QUILT COVER

23 cm (9 in)

25 cm (10 in)

A	B	A	C	A	B	A
C	A	B	A	C	A	B
A	C	A	B	A	C	A
B	A	C	A	B	A	C
A	B	A	C	A	B	A
C	A	B	A	C	A	B
A	C	A	B	A	C	A
B	A	C	A	B	A	C
A	B	A	C	A	B	A
C	A	B	A	C	A	B

SINGLE BED QUILT COVER

2 Pin, then machine-stitch the squares together in horizontal rows, right sides facing, taking 1.5 cm (⅝ in) seams. Press seams open.

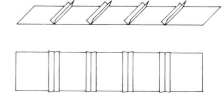

3 Pin, then machine-stitch the rows together, taking 1.5 cm (⅝ in) seams, making sure you have them in the correct order, to make the completed quilt cover front. Press seams open.

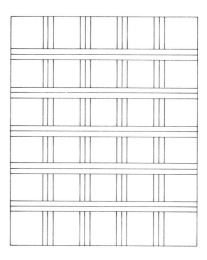

4 Continue from step 2 of Making a duvet cover, above, using the patchwork front and the backing fabric as though they were the front and back of a plain cover.

Making a comforter
To make a comforter 140 × 100 cm (56 × 40 in)

You will need

A piece of cotton fabric for the front 143 × 103 cm (57¼ × 41¼ in)
A piece of thick polyester wadding the same size

A piece of backing fabric the same size
Very narrow ribbon to co-ordinate with
    cover
A sharp needle with an eye large enough to
    take the ribbon.

1   Mark the positions for the ribbons on the
    front of the quilt cover with tailor's chalk.

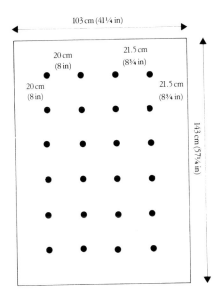

103 cm (41¼ in)

20 cm (8 in)   21.5 cm (8¾ in)

20 cm (8 in)   21.5 cm (8¾ in)

143 cm (57¼ in)

2   Lay out the quilt front face up, lay the
    backing on it face down and lay the
    wadding on top. Tack around the seam
    line, 1.5 cm (⅝ in) in from the raw edge,
    then trim the wadding close to the
    tacking. Machine along the tacking line,
    through all thicknesses, leaving an
    opening at the bottom edge. Clip the
    corners; trim wadding close to stiching.

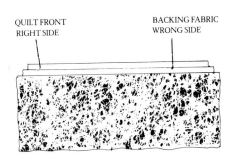

QUILT FRONT
RIGHT SIDE

BACKING FABRIC
WRONG SIDE

WADDING

3   Turn right side out through the opening,
    poking out the corners carefully. Press.
    Slip-stitch opening closed. Tack all layers
    together as shown.

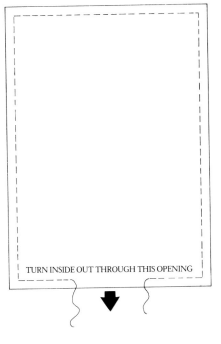

TURN INSIDE OUT THROUGH THIS OPENING

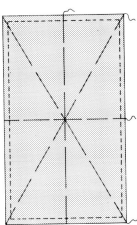

TACKING LAYERS TOGETHER

4   Cut 24 pieces of ribbon each 25 cm (10 in)
    long. Thread through the needle one at a
    time and sew from the front to the back
    on each dot, taking a small stitch and
    bringing back to the front. Tie in a small
    bow. Sew each knot in place with fine
    thread.

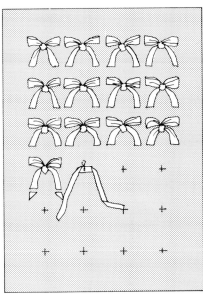

ALTERNATIVES TO BOWS

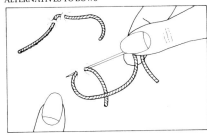

*Instead of using ribbon, quilt ties can
be made from appropriately coloured
cotton yarn.*

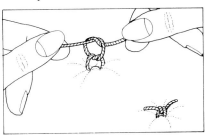

*Make a back stitch, using a needle
with a large eye, then tie in a (proper!)
reef knot.*

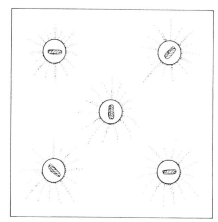

Instead of bows you can use buttons. Be sure to sew them on securely with strong thread.

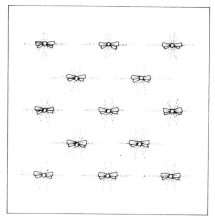

Quilt ties do not have to be in straight lines, you can stagger them instead as shown.

Making an album cot quilt

An album quilt is a delightful traditional American idea to which everyone you know, who is prepared to, can contribute two or three squares. For a more homogeneous look, you can advise them on your colour scheme if you like, or even supply them with the basic fabric square to work on. It is also the sort of thing that can easily be sent by post. Once the child has outgrown the cot the quilt can be hung on the wall in pride of place. Squares can be decorated with appliqué, embroidery or a combination of the two.

Choose all one colour for the squares (preferably white or a pale colour), choose an alternating chequerboard pattern, or have a random mixture of related colours.

To make a quilt 138 × 108 cm (55¼ × 43¼ in)

You will need

63 × 18 cm (7¼ in) squares of fine cotton fabric
Plain and patterned fabric of the same weight for appliqué
Embroidery cotton
A piece of thin polyester wadding 138 × 108 cm (55¼ × 43¼ in)
A piece of backing fabric for the quilt 138 × 108 cm (55¼ × 43¼ in)
2 strips of fabric 6 cm (2½ in) wide by 141 cm (56⅜ in) long and 2 strips 111 cm (44⅜ in) long to bind the edge of the quilt

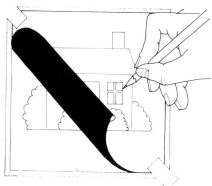

To transfer a design onto fabric you can use dressmaker's carbon paper.

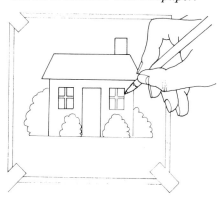

Then go over the design with a fabric marker pen or pencil to reinforce the lines.

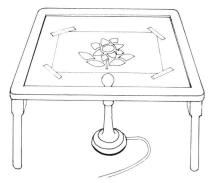

A design can be traced directly through fine fabric using an improvised 'light box'.

1 Ask people to decorate the squares with motifs and pictures, allowing a 1.5 cm (⅝ in) seam allowance all round. (For how to do appliqué see page 112, for suitable embroidery stitches see below). Children's drawings can make lovely designs too. Birds, ships, flowers, butterflies, houses, people, animals, nursery rhyme scenes, fruit and abstract shapes, letters of the alphabet (see page 103) are all suitable. The church where the child was christened, the town where he was born, the house where he lives and his favourite toys are also fine.

2 When you have all the squares back, arrange them in the form of a rectangle seven squares wide by nine long.

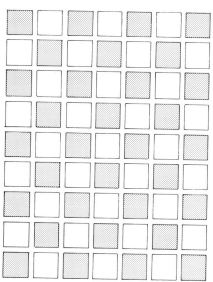

3 Pin, then machine-stitch the squares together in horizontal rows, right sides facing, taking 1.5 cm (⅝ in) seams. Press seams open. (See instructions for making a patchwork duvet cover on page 100).

4 Pin, then machine-stitch the rows together taking ⅝ in (1.5 cm) seams, making sure you have them in the correct order, to make the completed quilt cover front. Press seams open.

5 Make a sandwich with the quilt top on the top, right side out, then the wadding, then the backing fabric right side out.

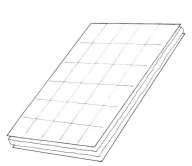

6 Tack round the edges of the quilt, across both centres and along the diagonals through all thicknesses. *For reference, see next page*.

Right: These two squares are taken from a late 19th century American embroidered album quilt in the American Museum in Britain. The quilt shows superb examples of naive design and such exhibits in galleries and museums can provide wonderful inspiration for our own craft work, as well as reassuring the less confident that artistic talent is not essential to obtain very charming results.

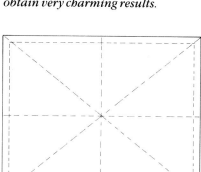

7   Machine-quilt through all thicknesses along the seam lines.

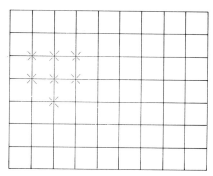

8   Bind the edges of the quilt as for the quilted rug in Chapter 3. Remove tacking.

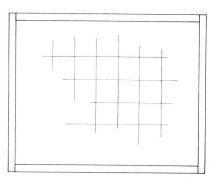

EMBROIDERY STITCHES FOR ALBUM QUILT

CHAIN STITCH

BACK STITCH

STEM STITCH

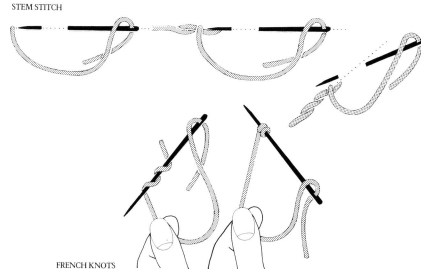

FRENCH KNOTS

8

ACCESSORIES

Accessories are the finishing touches in a room — the little things that make it special. They bring extra colour, make the room more interesting and create extra focal points for the child.

Accessories, such as nappy stackers, lined baskets, cushion covers, mobiles, toy tidy bags and framed pictures are available ready-made. But none of these are difficult to make yourself and by doing so you can choose

fabrics and materials that will link in with the room scheme and can also reflect an older child's interests.

By changing accessories, you can quickly update a room.

MOBILES

Mobiles provide movement to attract a baby's or child's attention. Hang one over your baby's cot or bed and one over the area where you change him. As a newborn baby's eyes are very sensitive to movement and cannot focus on anything much more than about 30 cm (12 in) away, a mobile is more exciting for him at that time than even the

best-planned and most imaginative colour scheme.

You can buy mobiles, some of which are clockwork and play soothing tunes as the figures revolve, to help the child get off to sleep. However, even the most basic mobile will amuse a small child. The simplest idea is simply to tie objects such as balloons, small

lightweight toys or strips of tissue paper on to a wire coat hanger and suspend it above the cot.

More elaborate mobiles can be suspended from thin strips of cane (such as are sold as supports for plants) or wire, suspended from each other using transparent nylon fishing line. Cut out cardboard shapes, paint them

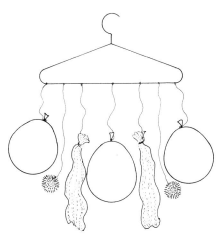

A coat hanger, tissue paper, balloons and pompoms make a cheap but effective mobile.

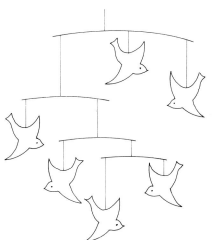

To make this bird mobile, cut out six bird shapes from thick card or fine ply and make a thread hole in each one at the point of balance (experiment on a spare shape). Hang the birds on the wire supports, adjusting their positions until balanced.

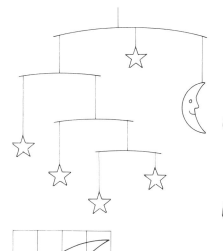

Imaginary animals, abstract shapes, hearts and fishes are all shapes that can be used for mobiles. If you are feeling creative try thinking up some unusual ones of your own.

This moon and stars mobile, with its obviously nocturnal theme, is made in the same way as the bird mobile. Spray the shapes gold and silver for extra impact.

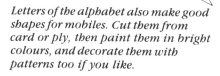

Letters of the alphabet also make good shapes for mobiles. Cut them from card or ply, then paint them in bright colours, and decorate them with patterns too if you like.

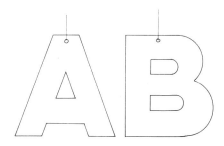

with poster colour or gouache and suspend them from the supports as shown. It is important to balance the mobile and to make sure the shapes will not crash into each other or become entangled as it goes round.

Safety note: Unless you buy a mobile or other cot toy that is intended to be within a child's grasp, always hang mobiles well out of the reach of the child and make sure they are

securely fixed to the ceiling, or whatever they are hanging from. It could be very dangerous if a mobile fell on to a baby.

A zany mobile cut from thick, painted card shapes creates a focal point in this room. Stencilling has also been carried out on the bed, chest of drawers and toy chest, which adds another very personal touch.

CUSHIONS

Besides making life more comfortable, cushions are also a great opportunity to introduce pattern and accent colour (see Colour scheming, Chapter 1) into a child's room. They also introduce colour and pattern in a way that is easy to change should you wish to alter the room scheme at a later date.

For children's rooms there is no point making complicated cushions, for example, with frills or piping round the edge, unless you really want to. The colours and patterns are what matters most; frills and piping are not only time consuming to apply, but they also make washing and ironing more complicated. Where piping is useful, however, is where a cushion or cover is for sitting on: then piping helps strengthen the seams. (see Making a simple chair cover, Chapter 6).

Cushion covers only need small amounts of fabric so you can use up remnants from curtains, bed covers etc. or, as you will not need much, you may like to splash out on a very special fabric. A mixture of cushions in a variety of carefully chosen plain colours can look stunning, and is the simplest proposition of all. Cushions are also a good size for experimenting with patchwork, appliqué, embroidery and fabric painting. If you want to make things even less daunting, you need only to make one side, and the other can be plain, co-ordinating backing fabric.

Cushion covers for children's rooms should ideally be made from medium-weight cotton fabric that will stand up to repeated washing. For this reason too, cushion covers should be easy to remove from the inner pad.

Cushions should always be made in the form of a cover and an inner pad, otherwise you will not be able to wash the cover. It is a good idea to wash the cover fabric before making it up, to be sure it will not shrink in future washes. This is also important with fabrics used for appliqué work as any loose dye is washed out then and is not likely to cause annoying cross-staining when washed.

For children's rooms, polyester fibre-filled pads are best. They are light, washable, non-allergic and comfortable. The pads can be machine washed and tumble dried. Never dry clean as the fibres absorb toxic fumes from the cleaning fluid. Cushion pads are available ready-made, or you can buy polyester fibre and use it to fill pad covers made from calico or sheeting. You will need about 450 gm (1 lb) fibre to fill a 38 cm (15¼ in) square pad cover.

Feather-filled pads, on the other hand, are best avoided for children's rooms. This type of filling must be dry cleaned, can smell unpleasant and cause allergies, and the older the feathers get, the more they are likely to crumble and become dusty and also to lose their resilience. So do not be tempted to recycle feathers from old quilts, cushions or pillows. Avoid foam chip fillings too as they tend to crumble and become lumpy and uncomfortable.

Making a square cushion

○ Make paper patterns from square paper to help you cut out the fabric pieces accurately.
○ Alternatively cut on a squared cutting board. It is very important that the fabric pieces are cut square (i.e. all corners are exact right angles), otherwise the finished cushion will be misshapen.
○ Press any creases out of the fabric before you cut it.

Making a cushion pad

(If you are buying your pads ready-made, miss out this section.)

You will need

One piece of calico or sheeting 79 × 41 cm (31⅛ × 16⅜ in)
About 450 g (1 lb) polyester fibre (you will need to experiment)
Glass-headed pins (safer to use than ordinary pins which could get lost in the cushion)
Ruler
Sewing machine
Dressmaking shears
Plastic point-turner (optional, from sewing shops)
Thread to match fabric

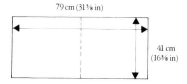

1 Fold the fabric in half, right sides together, to form a square. Taking a 1.5 cm (⅝ in) seam allowance, sew along the two sides nearest the fold, then turn the corner and sew a further 2 cm (¾ in) into each end of the fourth side to leave an opening.

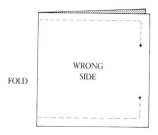

2 Clip off the corners to make turning inside out easier (do not cut into your stitching), then turn the cover right sides out, poking out the corners carefully with the points of a closed pair of scissors or, preferably, a plastic point turner which is less likely to damage the fabric. Press.

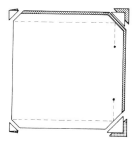

OVERSEWING THE OPENING

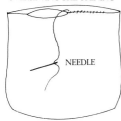

NEEDLE

3 Stuff with polyester fibre. To make cleaning up afterwards easiest, is best to do this in the (dry!) bath with the plug in. Wear an overall too, so that the fibres do not stick to your clothes. Fill the pad well, but do not over-stuff it so it becomes hard. Close the opening by machining or over-sewing by hand.

Making the cushion cover

There are two types of cushion cover most suited to a child's room. One has an overlap opening and the other has a zipper opening. The overlap opening is quicker and simpler to make but it takes more fabric and the finished effect is not quite as neat as the zipper type. The zipper type uses less fabric but it takes a little longer to make and you will need a zip, plus a zipper foot for your sewing machine.

○ If you are using a patterned fabric with a large design on it, make sure that you centre the pattern.
○ Make sure you cut on the straight grain on the fabric.
○ Pin then tack each seam for best results, unless you are an experienced sewer. Remove tacking once the cushion is finished.
○ Press the work at each stage.

Overlap opening

You will need

Cotton or cotton polyester fabric for the cover, either one piece 95 × 41 cm (38 × 16⅜ in) or one piece 41 cm (16⅜ in) square plus two pieces 41 × 30 cm (16⅜ × 12 in).
Glass-headed pins (safer to use than ordinary pins which could get lost in the cushion)

Ruler
Sewing machine
Dressmaking shears
Plastic point-turner (optional, from sewing shops)
Tailor's chalk or vanishing marker
Thread to match fabric
38 cm (15¼ in) square polyester fibre-filled pad

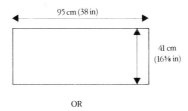

OR

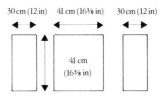

1 The simplest way to make this type of cushion is with one piece of fabric. However, if you want to use this method

RIGHT SIDE

WRONG SIDE

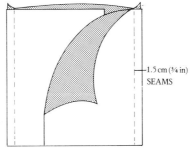

1.5 cm (¾ in) SEAMS

to make a cover incorporating a separate front panel, such as one made from patch-work or appliqué, or you are using up scraps of fabric and do not have a single piece 95 cm (38 in) long, you can make the cover in three pieces. The front is the 41 cm (16⅜ in) square piece and the two back pieces measure 41 × 30 cm (16⅜ × 12 in) each. Place the front on one of the back pieces, right sides together, lining up the 41 cm (16⅜ in) edges. Repeat on the other side. Tack along the seam lines then machine. Press the seams open then follow steps 2 to 5 above, as though you were working with just one piece of fabric.

1.5 cm (¾ in) FOLD

2 Turn both short edges under 1 cm (⅜ in) towards the wrong side, press, then turn under another 1.5 cm (⅝ in). Press, pin, tack, then machine these double hems.

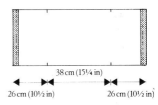

38 cm (15¼ in)

26 cm (10½ in)   26 cm (10½ in)

3 Staying on the wrong side, measure 26 cm (10⅜ in) from each end and mark this point in the seam line using chalk or a vanishing marker. If you have followed the instructions carefully the centre panel should measure 38 cm (15¼ in). If it does not, move the marks in or out until it does.

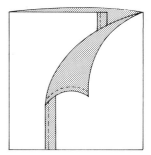

4 Turn to right side and fold in the ends at these points and press along the lines. The flaps should overlap by about 14 cm (5⅝ in).

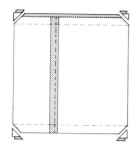

5 Make sure the top and bottom edges are all level, then tack along the top and bottom seam lines, 1.5 cm (⅝ in) in from the edges. Machine along these seam lines, through all thicknesses. Clip corners, making sure you do not cut the stitching. Turn right side through the overlap hole, poking out the corners carefully using a closed pair of scissors or a plastic point-turner. Press the cover, then carefully insert the pad (it may take a little manoeuvering).

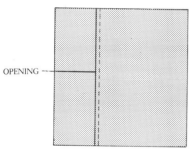

OPENING —

BACK VIEW OF FINISHED COVER

Zip opening
You will need

Cotton or cotton polyester fabric for the cover, two pieces 41 cm (16⅜ in) square
Zip — lightweight with 34 cm (13⅜ in) opening
Glass-headed pins (safer to use than ordinary pins which could get lost in the cushion)
Ruler
Sewing machine
Dressmaking shears

Plastic point-turner (optional, from sewing shops)
Tailor's chalk or vanishing marker
Thread to match fabric
38 cm (15¼ in) polyester fibre-filled pad

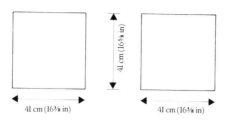

1 Place the squares of fabric together, right sides facing, and sew in 3.5 cm (1½ in) from either end along one side, taking a 1.5 cm (⅝ in) seam allowance. Tack the rest of the seam closed.

RIGHT SIDE

WRONG SIDE

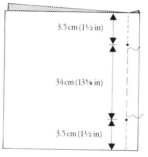

3.5 cm (1½ in)

34 cm (13⅜ in)

3.5 cm (1½ in)

2 Press the seam open. If the zip has been folded in the pack, iron it flat (avoid the teeth if it is a nylon zip as they may melt). Still working from the wrong side, centre the closed zip over the tacked seam. Pin in place, then tack along both long sides and across the ends just above the top stop of

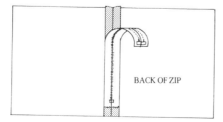

BACK OF ZIP

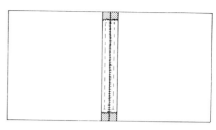

the zip (the bits of metal that stop the zip slider going any further) and just below the bottom stop.

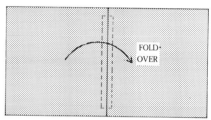

FOLD OVER

3 Change the foot on your sewing machine for a zipper foot and set the stitch for a medium-sized straight stitch. Working on the right side of the fabric, begin sewing from the top right hand corner of the zip, about 6 mm (¼ in) from the centre seam, with the zipper foot on the side of the needle away from the zip. Sew down the long side, stop at the bottom, pivot your sewing on the needle and sew along the bottom end of the zip. If you follow your tacking you will not sew over the end of the zip and break the needle. Pivot at the other corner, carry on up the other long side, pivot at the next corner and meet up with where you started. Pull the threads through to the back and tie them off. Take out the tacking and open the zip enough to enable you to turn the cushion right sides out when you have finished.

Gingham cushions and a pretty patchwork throw transform a divan bed into a wonderful place to sit and gaze. Throws are useful for livening up rather dull-looking pieces of upholstery too, and provide a comfy surface to sit on.

Safety note: small babies should not be left propped up on cushions unattended, and make sure that accessible windows have locks or bars.

4 Fold the fabric in half, right sides together, to form a square. Taking a 1.5 cm (⅝ in) seam allowance, pin, tack then sew along the three remaining side seams. Clip corners, making sure you do not cut the stitching. Turn right side out through the zip opening, poking out the corners carefully using a closed pair of scissors or a plastic point-turner. Press the cover, open the zip fully, then insert the pad and zip up.

ZIP OPENING

Of course you can make square cushions to any size. Just remember to make the finished cushion cover the same size as the pad, and allow for 1.5 cm (⅝ in) seam allowance all round. If you opt for a zip closer, buy a zip 4 cm (1⅝ in) shorter than the finished side length of the cushion. You can also try experimenting with other shapes of cushions — rectangular, triangular, circular and so on. You will need to work out the best position for the zip, to make sure you can get the pad in and out, and in the case of unusual shaped cushions you will need to make the pad yourself too. With circular cushions, the best position for the zip is across the centre of the back. Cut a paper pattern for the back (remembering to allow 1.5 cm (⅝ in) seam allowance all round) and cut it in half, adding a 1.5 cm (⅝ in) seam allowance to the cut edges. Buy a zip 5.5 cm (2¼ in) shorter than the length of this centre line and sew it in place, following instructions for the zipped cushion. Then sew the front to the back.

IDEAS FOR DECORATING THE FRONTS OF SQUARE CUSHIONS

Appliqué

Appliqué involves sewing coloured patches of cloth on to a backing fabric to form a pattern or a pictorial motif. Designing your own motifs is fun and you can find inspiration in children's pictures and colouring books, and from wallpaper and fabrics. If you are a beginner then choose a simple design with mostly straight lines and some gentle curves. Avoid patterns with lots of fiddly pieces or with sharp pointed motifs as these are difficult to sew.

Choose fabrics for the motifs that will not fray easily. Avoid felt though, as it wears quickly and is not washable. You can either construct a motif from pieces of different coloured fabric, or you can cut motifs ready-made from printed fabric. The appliqué fabric should be the same type of fibre and a similar weight to the backing fabric. Medium-weight cotton is ideal. Wash fabrics first to shrink and prevent cross-dying from non-fast fabric.

Although it is possible to appliqué by hand, it means using quite fine fabrics and the end result is not very durable. Machine appliqué is better for children's rooms because it is stronger. You will need a machine that will do zig-zag stitch, and you may need to practice a little first.

You will need

41 cm (16⅜ in) square of medium-weight cotton backing fabric for the cushion cover front
Scraps of coloured medium-weight cotton fabric for the appliqué motifs
Paper to draw design out on
Tracing paper
Thin card (optional)
Pins
Coloured pencils, tailor's chalk pencil or vanishing marker
Dressmaker's carbon paper (optional)
Small sticky labels
Fine thread or machine embroidery cotton in colours to match design

1 Draw out the design full-size and the way up it is going to appear on the cushion cover. Where shapes overlap indicate the outline of the underlying shapes with dotted lines. Number and write the colour on each shape, draw a vertical line through each piece (so you can line it up with the grain of the fabric when you come to cut out — having the grain of all the pieces running in the same direction helps eliminate puckering and distortion). If you are following the teddy bear design shown here and you want to avoid small, fiddly pieces you can make a simplified version by just cutting out body, trousers and mouth oval. You can mark in the eyes and nose with hand embroidery or a black fabric dye pen.

1 sq = 6 cm

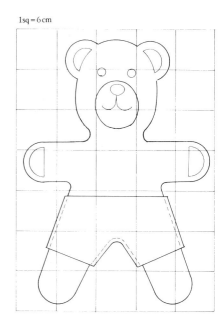

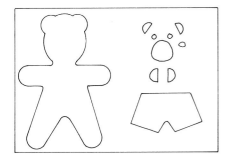

2 Trace off each complete shape on to tracing paper, mark on all information from the original drawing, then cut your tracing apart to use as paper patterns. For machine appliqué you do not need to add seam allowances or turnings to appliqué pieces. If you are going to cut several pieces from each pattern, stick the pattern on to thick card and cut out.

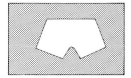

3 Place the pattern or template right side up on the right side of the correct fabric for that piece. Line up the vertical grain of the fabric with the vertical grain line that you have drawn on the pattern. If you are using templates, draw round them on to the fabric, using a sharp coloured pencil similar in colour to the fabric, a tailor's chalk, pencil or a vanishing fabric marker. Cut out the pieces along the lines. If you are using paper patterns, pin them on and cut out round them.

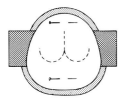

4 Trace any extra embroidery lines on to the front using dressmaker's carbon paper (you can only do this with paper patterns).

5 To distinguish the different pieces, if there are several, stick a small self-adhesive label on each piece showing the number of the piece. Stick it right way up and on the right side of the fabric for extra guidance.

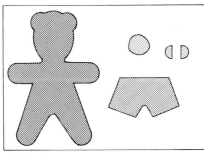

6 Mark the centre of the cushion cover, with coloured tacking thread, to make placing the motif easier. Rub a glue stick over the back of the pieces (check first that it will not show through on the front of the fabric), then arrange them in place, using your drawing for guidance, right side up on the right side of the fabric, overlapping the pieces if necessary. Add a few tacking stitches to hold the pieces firmly.

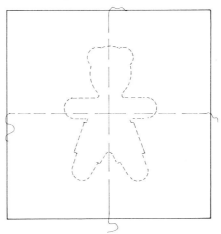

7 Put a sharp, new needle in your sewing machine. Work a row of straight machine stitching close to the edge of each piece of the motif.

8 Using fine sewing thread or machine embroidery thread to contrast or match the design, set your machine to a half to full width zig-zag stitch and a short

stitch length. Some machines have an appliqué foot with wide prongs and a groove underneath, so use that in preference to a zig-zag foot if your machine has one. Centre the needle over the raw edge and satin-stitch to cover the machine-stitching and the edge. Work slowly and carefully so that you are in complete control. Adjust the stitch length to get a solid line, but not so much that it makes a very slow, heavy stitch. On curves raise and lower the presser foot often so that you do not get a jerky line. If you are new to appliqué, practise on scrap fabric first, with as many layers and the types of shapes used on the proper item. Test the zig-zag stitch first and experiment to get the best length and width.

9 Add extra embroidery on top of the motif, either by machine or by hand, to create extra details.

10 Remove tacking stitches and make the finished square up into a cushion cover following the instructions on p 109–110.

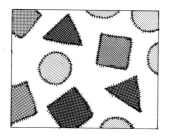

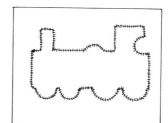

Other ideas for appliqué cushion covers

○ Cut out simple geometric shapes and arrange in a random pattern. Where shapes overlap the edge of the cover square, simply trim off the excess.

○ Children's drawings and paintings often make a delightful source of original design. Here a 41 cm (16⅜ in) square for the background was made by sewing a piece of blue and white spotted cotton fabric (representing the sky) measuring 41 × 26.5 cm (16⅜ × 10⅜ in) to a piece of green and white spotted cotton fabric (representing the ground) measuring 41 × 17.5 cm (16⅜ × 7 in), seam. The cat motif was cut from brown and beige striped cotton fabric and sewn on to the background. Mouth and whiskers were machine embroidered, nose and eyes were hand embroidered.

○ Appliquéing motifs from printed fabric: cut round the edge of the motif using small sharp needlework scissors. Sew to fabric following points above for ordinary appliqué, using a thread to match the background fabric.

For full instructions on appliqué, see page 112.

PATCHWORK CUSHION COVERS

If a variety of fabrics are used for patchwork, they must be the same weight, fabric type, texture and strength.

Four strip patchwork

A very simple idea perfect for beginners, this looks best in a mixture of bright colours or prints. Combine four colours from the room scheme for a really co-ordinated effect.

You will need

To make a front cushion panel for a 38 cm (15¼ in) cushion pad (make two if you want an identical front and back)
Four pieces of medium-weight cotton fabric each measuring 41 × 12.5 cm (16⅜ × 5 in) and each in a different colour

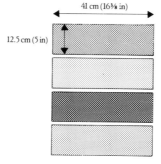

41 cm (16⅜ in)

12.5 cm (5 in)

1 Lay out your four pieces of fabric, right side up and long sides together, so that you can see which order they look best in.

2 Pin the pieces together, right sides together, taking 1.5 cm (⅝ in) seam allowance. Machine-stitch and press the seams open.

WRONG SIDE

3 If you are making the front and back of the cover the same, use a zip fastening (see page 110). If you are opting for a plain back you can choose either a zip or overlap opening (see pages 109–110).

Simple patchwork squares

As there are various combinations possible with this design, work out some ideas on paper first.

You will need

To make a front cushion panel for a 38 cm (15¼ in) cushion pad (make two if you want an identical front and back) you will need 12 squares of medium-weight cotton fabric each 9.5 cm (3¾ in) square, in a variety of colours and prints.

1 Assemble the squares to make the required pattern, as with the previous design (above).

2 Make four lines of four patches: pin and tack the pieces together, taking a 1.5 cm (⅝ in) seam allowance. Machine-stitch and press seams open.

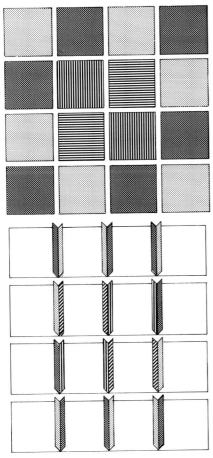

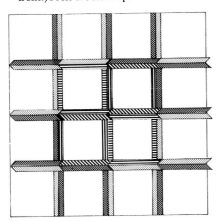

3 Again, arrange the strips on the table to make sure you have them in the right order. Then sew these strips together, making sure you have the right sides facing (it is easy to get in a muddle and find you have sewn a strip in back to front!) Press the seam open.

4 If you are making the front and back of the cover the same, use a zip fastening (see page 110). If you are opting for a plain back you can choose either a zip or overlap opening (see pages 109–110)

Right: Choose a mixture of strongly patterned and contrastingly coloured fabrics for really vibrant patchwork cushion covers. Even more exciting is to appliqué different designs and patterns onto the squares. Be sure to wash the fabrics first though so that colours do not bleed later and spoil your handiwork, and to make sure fabrics are all preshrunk.

Making shaped novelty cushions

Simple animal shapes, with a little embroidery or appliqué to give essential details, can make a comfy cushion which also has the appeal of a stuffed toy. Because of the irregular shape of these designs, it is not possible to have a separate inner pad. But so long as you choose a washable fabric and use polyester fibre to stuff them with, an occasional sponge-over with soapy suds or even a full-scale wash, either by hand of in the machine, should present no problems.

You will need

Fabric for the cover
Extra fabric scraps of the same weight for appliqué
Polyester fibre for filling
Embroidery thread either for hand or machine embroidery

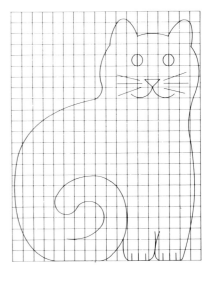

1 Draw up the pattern on to squared paper and add a 1.5 cm (⅜ in) seam allowance all round. Cut out identical front and back shapes and embroider and/or appliqué on the details. You can draw directly on to

1 square = 2 cm

EMBROIDER DETAILS
WITH CHAIN STITCH

1 Make a paper pattern of the size of foam you need and take it to a foam shop. Ask them to cut a piece of combustion modified high resilience (CMHR) foam to that size: tell the shop assistant what you want the foam for as there are different densities for different uses. You can make a fibre-filled shaped cushion instead — this will need to have boxed sides as well. To make the pad follow the instructions for making the outer cover but omit the piping and zip. Simply leave an opening which you stuff with polyester fibre and then oversew closed.

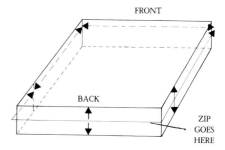

FRONT

BACK

ZIP
GOES
HERE

2 Cut a top and a bottom piece for the cushion, 1.5 cm (⅝ in) bigger all round than the foam or pad.

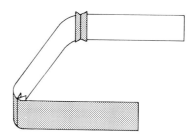

3 Measure all round the cushion. Cut a side gusset the depth of the cushion plus 3 cm (1¼ in), by the length of the zip plus 3 cm (1¼ in). Cut another gusset piece to the same depth, by the distance round the length of the cushion minus the length of the zip but plus 3 cm (1¼ in) for seams.

4 Insert the zip as for the zipped cushion, taking a 1.5 cm (⅝ in) seam allowance

the fabric using tailor's chalk or a vanishing cloth marker, or you can trace from the pattern on to the fabric using dressmaker's carbon paper.

2 Sew the front to the back, right sides facing, leaving a gap for inserting the filling. Turn right sides out, clipping corners and trimming seam allowances if necessary. Poke out any corners carefully using a closed pair of scissors or a point-turner.

3 Fill generously, but not so the cushion is hard. You may find that poking the filling into tight corners, such as ears, is made easier by using a blunt pencil. Slip-stitch the opening closed.

Making box cushions

A box cushion is simple to make and can transform a wicker arm chair or a toy box into a comfy place to sit.

You will need

CMHR foam cut to size (see below) or polyester fibre plus cambric for cover
Fabric for covering
Fabric for making bias binding, plus piping cord (see Chapter 6, Making a simple chair cover)
Zip fastener — this should be long enough to go across the back of the cushion, plus extending 7 cm (2¾ in) round each side.

and having the fabric extending 1.5 cm (⅝ in) at either end of the zip.

5 Join the short ends of this piece to the short ends of the gusset piece, right sides together and taking a 1.5 cm (⅝ in) seam allowance. This should form a continuous loop of fabric. Press seams open.

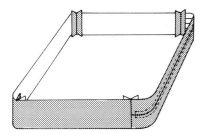

6 Prepare enough covered piping to go around the top and bottom of the cover (see Chapter 6, Making a simple chair cover).

7 Attach the piping to the top and bottom edges of the gusset strip, right sides together, having raw edges level. Tack then machine in place using a zipper foot.

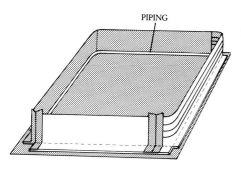

PIPING

8 Pin the top piece to the gusset, right sides together, raw edges level, taking a 1.5 cm (⅝ in) seam allowance. Clip into the seam allowance is necessary to allow the fabric to lie flat. Tack then machine in place.

9 Open the zip, then repeat the last stage for the bottom. Remove the tacking, then press the seams towards the gusset.

10 Turn right sides out through the zip and insert the cushion pad.

OTHER ACCESSORIES

Lining baskets

Simple wicker can be made to look very special by lining them with fabric. They can then be used for holding cotton wool balls, cotton buds, nappy pins and other items.

You will need

A basket to line
Fabric for lining it
Narrow bias binding
Ribbon

1 For a shallow, bowl-shaped basket, press tissue paper inside to make a pattern and cut a circle or oval of the fabric in a corresponding size. Trim the edge with bias binding, machining it in place on the right side and folding over the wrong side and slip-stitching it in place.

2 For a basket with a flat base and sloping sides, make a pattern of the base and add 1.5 cm (⅝ in) all round. Measure the depth of the sloping sides and add 1.5 cm (⅝ in). Measure the circumference of the top of the basket and add 3 cm (1¼ in). Cut a piece of fabric to this depth and length, and join the short ends, right sides together, taking a 1.5 cm (⅝ in) seam.

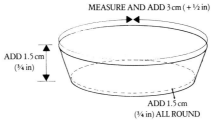

MEASURE AND ADD 3 cm (+ ½ in)

ADD 1.5 cm (¾ in)

ADD 1.5 cm (¾ in) ALL ROUND

3 Run a gathering thread around the bottom edge, draw it up until it is the length of the seam line on the base. Make sure the gathers are even.

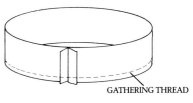

GATHERING THREAD

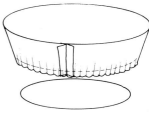

4 Pin the sides to the base, tack then machine in place. Remove the gathers and tacking, then trim the seam. Press.

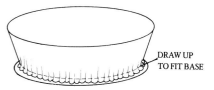

DRAW UP TO FIT BASE

5 Trim the top edge of the fabric with bias binding as before.

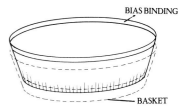

BIAS BINDING

BASKET

6 If the baskets have handles you can add ribbon ties to the linings and tie them round the handles to hold them in place.

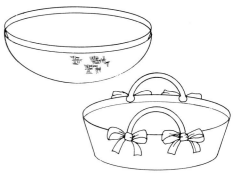

Coat hanger covers

Covered coat hangers look very pretty and are ideal for hanging special clothes on.

You will need

A wooden child-size coat hanger
Fabric for covering
Medium polyester wadding
Ribbon

1   Cut a piece of fabric and a piece of wadding 14 cm (5⅝ in) deep and 6 cm (2⅜ in) longer than the hanger. Tack them together 1 cm (½ in) in from the edges.

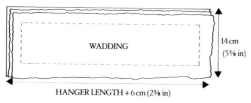

WADDING

14 cm (5⅝ in)

HANGER LENGTH + 6 cm (2⅜ in)

2   Trim 6 mm (¼ in) wadding from both long edges then turn the fabric down over the edge of the wadding and tack in place.

WADDING

WADDING

3   Fold the fabric in half lengthways, right sides facing and use a small glass or compass to draw a semi-circle about 6 mm (¼ in) in from each end.

4   Machine along the semi-circles then trim fabric close to stitching.

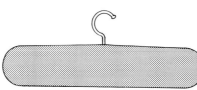

5   Turn right side out, press, then insert the hanger.
6   Sew the top edges together with tiny stitches, gathering up the fabric to fit.

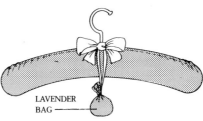

LAVENDER BAG

Finish off with a ribbon bow at the base of the hook. You can also hang a small matching bag of lavender or pot-pourri from the hook.

Nappy stacker

A nappy stacker is an attractive and handy way to store terry nappies and you can hang it in a convenient place just above the changing area.

You will need

A child's wooden coat hanger 36 cm (14⅜ in) wide (cut a wooden one down if necessary)
Two pieces of fabric 33 × 24 cm (13¼ × 9⅝ in)
A piece of firm iron-on interfacing 30 × 21 cm (12 × 8⅜ in) for the base

A piece of stiff cardboard 30 × 21 cm (12 × 8⅜ in) for the base
Fabric glue
A piece of fabric 33 cm (13¼ in) wide by 50 cm (20 in) high for the back
Two pieces of fabric 24 cm (9⅝ in) wide by 50 cm (20 in) high for sides
Two pieces of fabric 16.5 cm (6⅝ in) wide by 50 cm (20 in) high for the front
Two pieces of 4 cm (1⅝ in) bias binding, each 50 cm (20 in) long
Two pieces of fabric 33 cm (13¼ in) wide by 12 cm (4⅝ in) deep
Two pieces of firm iron-on interfacing 33 cm (13¼ in) by 12 cm (4⅝ in) deep for the top
Ribbon

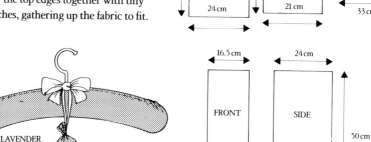

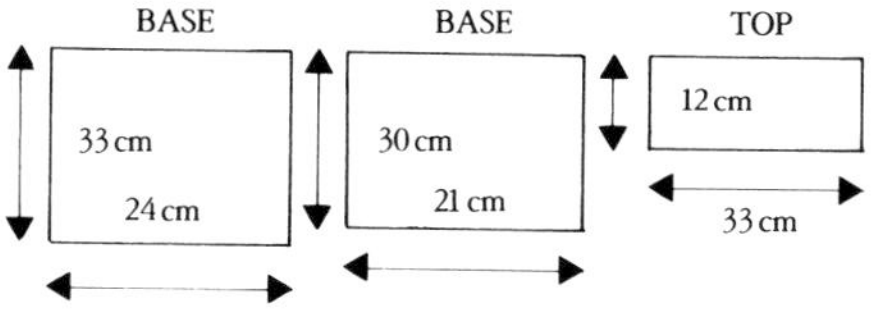

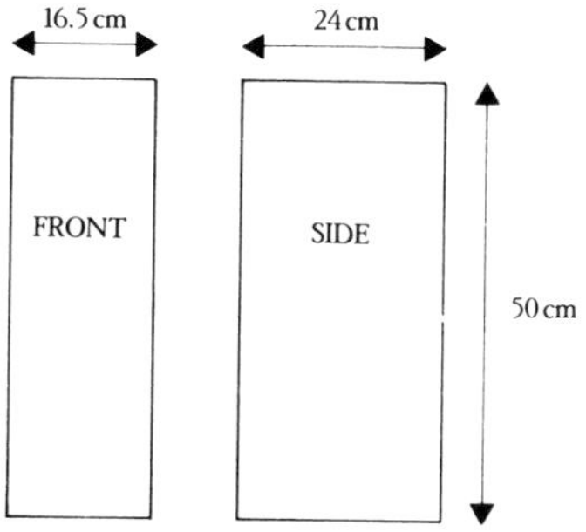

BASE	BASE	TOP
33 cm / 24 cm	30 cm / 21 cm	12 cm / 33 cm

16.5 cm — FRONT

24 cm — SIDE

50 cm

33 cm — BACK — 50 cm

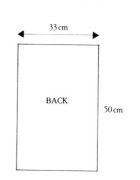

Matching accessories are the finishing touch for a room. These are available ready-made, but if you have time and would like to have a go at making your own it is not difficult.

1 Bind the two long inside edges of the front with the bias binding taking a 1 cm (⅜ in) seam (see Chapter 6, page 60 for how to bind edges of fabric). (See right).

2 Sew the left front, left side, back, right side and right front together, right sides together, taking a 1.5 cm (⅝ in) seam, but do not sew beyond the corner of the seam line in each case. (See below).

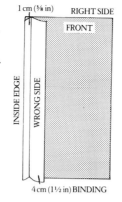
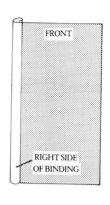

3 Iron the interfacing on to the wrong side of one piece of the base fabric, centring it on the fabric.

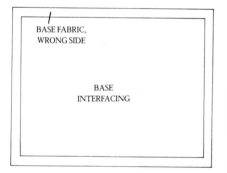

4 Pin the sides, back and front on to the base, right sides together, taking a

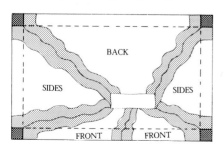

1.5 cm (⅝ in) seam allowance, butting up the front edges and opening out the corner seam allowances. Tack, then sew, pivoting the machine needle on each corner. Turn right sides out and press.

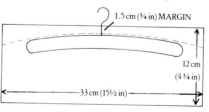

5 Cut a piece of paper 33 × 12 cm (13¼ × 4⅝ in) and lay the coat hanger on it, positioning the topmost edge of the wooden part 1.5 cm (⅝ in) down from the top of the paper, and making sure the hanger is level. Draw along the top edge of the hanger. Take away the hanger and

add 1.5 cm (⅝ in) seam allowance above this line. Cut along this second line and use this piece of paper as a pattern to cut the upper edges of the two pieces of fabric 33 × 12 cm (13¼ × 4⅝ in). Also cut the two pieces of interfacing, making them 1.5 cm (⅝ in) smaller all round.

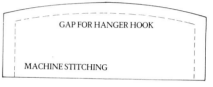

6 Iron the interfacing on to the backs of the fabric pieces, centring them.

7 Join these two pieces, omitting the bottom edge and leaving a small gap at the top centre for the hanger hook to pass through. Trim seam, clip curves, turn right side out and press.

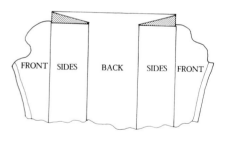

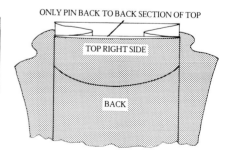

8 Join the lower part of the stacker to the top part. Take the lower part and pleat the side panels in half, so that the corner

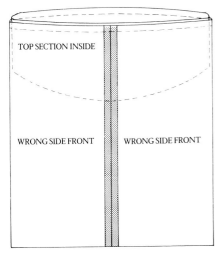

TOP SECTION INSIDE

WRONG SIDE FRONT   WRONG SIDE FRONT

seams are together. Tack these pleats to the back panel along the top seam allowance. Turn the lower part inside out, pin the top part (right way out), upside down to the top edge of the back of the lower part. Only pin to one side of the top part. Fold the front panels round and pin these to the other side of the top part butting front edges and with raw edges even. Tack, then machine.

9 Turn right side out through front slot and insert the coat hanger.

10 Cover the piece of card with the other piece of fabric 33 × 24 cm (13¼ × 9⅝ in) and stick the fabric down on the back with fabric glue. Allow to dry, then place in the bottom of the stacker. Tie a ribbon around the base of the hook.

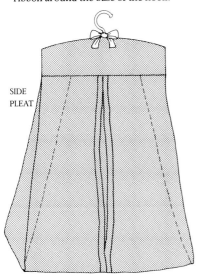

SIDE
PLEAT

PICTURES FOR NURSERIES

Pictures bring a room to life, and children love to be surrounded by favourite images. Ready-made frames have made this much easier and cheaper, and the things you frame do not have to be expensive either. Children's own drawings and paintings look extra special once framed, as do posters, photographs, postcards and pictures from magazines and old children's books. When the child out-grows these images, just ask him to choose something else to slip in the frame instead.

You can also make special paintings for children, showing their names, with each letter combined with objects that begin with the same letter. If you do feel confident about designing something yourself you can always trace off motifs from other sources or even make up a collage from magazine pictures, and use rub-down lettering for the letters.

A personalized name picture makes a very special addition to a child's room and will take pride of place on the wall for years to come, as well as having educational value.

You will need
A suitable sized ready-made frame (see below)
Heavy cartridge paper cut to fit in the frame
Watercolours, poster colours or gouache, or large-size rub-down lettering and collage material

1 Trace off the letters that spell out your child's name and space them out nicely, leaving enough space for decorating around them. Spacing out letters is not easy, so stand back, have a critical look and if you do not think they look quite right have another go. When you have got it right you can work out the size of frame that will look best for your picture.

2 Trace the letters on to the paper (go over the back of the tracing with pencil and then retrace your drawing on to the paper), making sure you have centred the lettering on the paper.

3 Paint in the letters, allowing your creativity free rein.

4 When it is dry, mount it in the frame.

ALPHABETICAL GUIDE TO SEWING EQUIPMENT

Although a bad workman is said to blame his tools, the truth is that if you want to make a good job of something, you really do need decent equipment, and this is just as true for sewing as for other activities. That does not mean that you need lots of complicated or expensive gadgets to start sewing, but simply that what you do have should be good quality, looked after carefully and replaced when necessary. It is a false economy to spend money on fabric, only to try to cut it up with blunt scissors and sew it with a blunt needle, for example. The following list is of the basic equipment that you will need to get going. You can build up your workbox over a period of time, buying extra things as and when you need them.

Beeswax Usually provided with a plastic holder, beeswax can be used to coat sewing threads with. It strengthens the thread and makes it much less likely to tangle, become knotted or break.

Needle threader A small gadget to make needle threading easier, especially useful if you have bad eyesight.

Pinking shears Shears with zig-zag blades used for neatening the edge of fabrics which do not unravel easily.

Piping cord Cotton cord which is encased in bias binding and used to decorate and strengthen seams. It can be used on cushions and loose covers. Piping cord may need shrinking before you use it, in which case follow the manufacturer's instructions. Piping comes in various thicknesses, buy the one that looks in best proportion to the item it is intended for.

Sewing gauge A small plastic or metal ruler with a sliding indicator, useful where you need to repeat the same measurement several times.

Sewing machine Sewing using a machine is much quicker than by hand and the resulting stitches are much stronger too. When choosing a machine, consider opting for one which also does zig-zag stitches and which has a free arm — this can make certain types of fiddly sewing much easier. Some machines will also do hemming and button holes, which is useful, but think carefully before opting for a machine which does lots of embroidery stitches — you may never use them.

T-square A wooden, plastic or metal tool for marking right-angles, also useful for finding the straight grain of fabric.

Tailor's chalk Use to mark sewing lines on fabric. Check that the chalk will brush off by testing it on a piece of scrap fabric first.

Thimble Although it takes a little getting used to, a thimble makes for quicker and more efficient sewing. Wear one on the middle finger of the hand you hold your needle in and use it to push the needle through the fabric.

Thread Available in different fibres, thicknesses and colours. Mercerized cotton is best for sewing on cotton fabric. Buy synthetic thread or a synthetic/cotton mixture for sewing on synthetics. Cotton-covered polyester thread is strong and can be used for sewing most fabrics. If you cannot find a thread to match the colour of a fabric choose a darker rather than a lighter shade, as it will show up less. With multi-coloured fabric, match the colour to the overall effect rather than the background colour.

Unpicker/seam ripper Very useful for quick unpicking of machine stitching.

A name picture is a lovely present for a child, and this one is particularly beautiful. Each letter has been teamed with an object that starts with the same character and it has been laid out very attractively.

SAFETY APPENDIX

Although this book is concerned with decorating and furnishing bedrooms for small children, there are certain safety factors which apply throughout the home when there are babies and small children around. As your child grows, different potential problems will suggest themselves. A walking child, for example, can reach higher than a crawling child, so try to think ahead and imagine problems that may arise, so you can be forearmed.

Many countries have standards and regulations governing safety requirements for baby products, but even so some standards are simply voluntary guidelines and unscrupulous shops may sell merchandise that does not conform to regulations. So when buying anything for babies and small children, purchase from reliable and reputable stores and manufacturers who have high safety standards.

GENERAL SAFETY

○ Keep polythene bags and all potentially poisonous substances locked away out of reach of small children. As well as the obvious things, don't forget paint, adhesives, alcohol, shoe polish, washing up liquid, washing powder and shampoo.
○ Doors leading outside, especially to roads or balconies, should have bolts or catches fitted out of reach of small children, and should be kept locked.
○ Once children can walk, do not leave keys in doors where children can lock themselves in or others out.
○ Don't put furniture near balcony railings; children could climb on to it and fall over the edge.
○ Keep floors tidy so there is nothing for children or adults to trip over or slip on.
○ Rugs should have non-slip backings and should be heavy enough to lie properly flat.
○ Floors should be kept clean – babies crawl around on them and then put their fingers into their mouths, and spills on smooth floors can become very slippery.
○ Electric flexes should be kept tidy and out of the way, clipping them to the wall with cable clips where possible. Use appliances as close to the socket as you can to minimize trailing cables. Babies may chew through wires, and toddlers may trip over them. Avoid table lamps for the same reasons.

○ Children may try to poke things, including their fingers, into electric sockets so either have sockets moved up the wall out of their reach or cover with inexpensive socket covers.
○ Furniture must be sturdy and stable as crawling babies will try to pull themselves up on it, and older children may climb on it. Where possible, fix it to the wall. A free-standing bookcase full of books, for example, falling on a child may well result in tragedy. Fitted furniture is safest, but as children love climbing in wardrobes and trunks, make sure doors are easy to open from the inside. Do not leave items of furniture, such as chairs, where they can be used to climb on to reach dangerous or fragile items.
○ Low windows, patio doors and conservatories should be made of laminated or toughened safety glass – stick colourful self-adhesive shapes on to these types of windows at children's eye level to prevent them bumping into the glass. Where it is not possible to replace ordinary glass, self-adhesive safety film is available from child-care stores. In the event of the glass breaking, it holds all the pieces together.
○ Windows should be fitted with window locks to prevent children climbing out. Some locks allow you to open a window a small amount without being able to push

it open any further. Children's bedroom windows can, if you prefer, be fitted with vertical window bars (children can climb up horizontal ones). These should be close enough together so that children can't get their heads stuck between them. They should be removeable by an adult in the event of a fire.
○ Smoke detectors make good sense and most models are quite inexpensive. Position them according to manufacturer's instructions. If you have a large house you may need more than one.

And although there are lots of gadgets around to make life safer for small children and less of a worry for parents, remember that these gadgets are not a substitute for proper supervision of your child. Kitchens and stairs are the main danger areas in the home for children, so be extra vigilant here.

In your child's bedroom
○ Fit bars and locks to windows and move furniture away from them so your child cannot use it to climb out.
○ Choose furniture with rounded edges, or fit plastic safety corners.
○ Do not put toys or games on high shelves where your child may try to climb up for them.
○ Always put the cot side up properly

when your baby is in the cot.

○ Do not leave your baby alone on the changing surface, ever.

○ Be sure that any paint you use is lead-free.

○ If you have cats or dogs, keep them out of small children's rooms, and make sure that your pets cannot open the door on their own.

In the living room

○ Put electrical equipment such as hi-fi equipment, videos and telephones above the 1.2 m (4 ft) 'toddler zone'.

○ If you must have a glass-topped table make sure it is laminated or toughened safety glass, and don't choose designs with sharp corners.

○ Do not leave sewing or knitting equipment lying around.

○ Move ornaments out of reach, and preferably out of sight so children won't be tempted to climb up and get them.

○ Never leave a child alone in a room with an unguarded fire; a fireguard must be used. It should be screwed to the wall and be far enough (at least 20 cm [8 in]) from the heat source so that it doesn't become hot. Never attempt to dry things on a fireguard – they may catch fire.

○ Never leave matches, lighters or alcohol where children can find them. Keep drinks cupboards locked – spirits are poisonous to small children.

In the dining room

○ When children are small it is unwise to use tablecloths – they can pull china, cutlery and hot food on to themselves.

In the kitchen

○ Never let electric leads hang over the edge of the worktop as children can pull electrical equipment and kettles of boiling water on to themselves – make sure you push the items well to the back of the worktop. For the same reason never leave irons (whether cold or hot) unattended. Curly leads are neater and are more likely to stay out of harm's way.

○ It is especially important to keep kitchen floors tidy and free from spills, especially oily or greasy ones.

○ Saucepans should, when possible, be put on the back rings of the hob. Always turn handles inwards. Cooker or hob guards can be used in addition to these precautions, but care must be taken as pans must be lifted over the guard or they may catch on it and spill.

○ Kitchen cupboards and drawers should lock, preferably, or have safety catches. Be especially vigilant about knives and other sharp tools, and keep cleaning materials and medicines locked away well out of reach. Although they are very useful, don't rely too much on plastic safety catches as children can sometimes break them or discover how they work.

○ Fridge-freezer catches prevent small children raiding the fridge – especially important if you tend to keep medicines or opened bottles of wine in there.

On the stairs

○ Once a child starts to crawl, fit metal or wooden safety gates at the top and bottom of any stairs. Gaps between the bars (which should be vertical so children

can't climb on them) should be no more than 8.5 cm (3½ in) wide.

○ Keep stairs clear of toys.

○ Check that stair carpet isn't worn and hasn't come loose anywhere.

○ For safety's sake, stairs must be well lit; but don't position lights so they shine into your eyes when you climb the stairs. Glowing plug-lights are useful to have on landings once children are old enough to find their own way to the bathroom in the middle of the night.

In the bathroom

○ Once your child is able to walk, replace door bolts with safety bathroom locks which can be opened from outside with a screwdriver.

○ Never leave a bath of water unattended when small children are around.

○ Turn your hot water thermostat down to 54°C (130°F) or lower and always run cold water in the bath first before turning on the hot tap.

○ Lock potential poisons such as medicines, bleach, perfume, cleaning materials, air-freshener blocks and shampoo out of reach. Do the same with sharp implements such as scissors and razor blades. Medicine cabinets should preferably lock, but don't forget to hide the key. If there is no lock, fit a safety catch.

○ Use a slip-resistant bath mat once your child graduates to the proper bath.

○ Supports that enable babies to sit up in an adult bath are available, but these must not be relied on as a safety aid. Do not leave a toddler alone in one even for a moment.

ADDRESSES

Akzo Nobel Decorative Coatings, Crown House, PO Box 37, Hollins Road, Darwen, Lancs BB3 0BG; tel: 01254 704951 – manufacturers of Anaglypta and other relief wallcoverings

Anna French, 343 Kings Road, London SW3 5ES; tel: 0171–351 1126 – children's fabrics, wallcoverings and bedlinen

Boots, 1 Thane Road West, Nottingham NG2 3AA; tel: 0115 9506111 – baby equipment, useful catalogue from stores or by post; contact for nearest store

Boras Cotton (UK), 4A Boardman Industrial Estate, Hearthcote Road, Swadlincote, Derbyshire DE11 9DL; tel: 01283 550011 – manufacturers of brightly coloured children's fabrics in modern designs

Britax Restmor, Restmor Way, Hackbridge Road, Wallington, Surrey SM6 7AQ; tel: 0181–669 4333 – manufacturers of nursery equipment

Bundles Designs, 222 Century Building, Brunswick Dock, Liverpool; tel: 0151–709 5595 – children's fabrics, bedlinen and wallpapers

Coates Crafts UK, The Lingfield Estate, PO Box 22, McMullan Road, Darlington, County Durham DL1 1YQ; tel: 01325 394237 – manufacturers and distributors of sewing and needlecraft equipment; contact for your nearest stockist

Cosatto, Wollaston Way, Burnt Mills, Basildon SS13 1LL; tel: 01268 727070 – manufacturers of prams, cots and highchairs

Cover Charm, Rainbow Fairweather Decorative Furniture, Unit 14 The Talina Centre, Bagleys Lane, London SW6 2BW; tel: 0171–736 1258 – manufacturers of radiator covers

Crown Paints Advice Centre, PO Box 37, Crown House, Hollins Road, Darwen, Lancs BB3 0BG; tel: 01254 704951 – paint manufacturer

Crown Wallcoverings, Belgrave Mills, Belgrave Road, Darwen, Lancs BB3 2RR; tel: 01254 704988 – manufacturers of children's wallcoverings and fabrics

Designers Guild, 271 and 277 Kings Road, London SW3 5EN; tel: 0171–351 5775 – children's fabric and wallcovering designs

Dulux Paints, ICI Paints Division, Wexham Road, Slough, Berks SL2 5DS; tel: 01753 31151 – paint and varnish manufacturer

Dunlopillo, Pannal, Harrogate, North Yorks HG3 1JL; tel: 01423 872411 – manufacturer of good quality latex foam mattresses

Dylon International, Worsley Bridge Road, London SE26 5HD; tel: 0181–650 4801 – manufacturers of home dyestuffs, fabric paints and fabric pens

Forbo-Nairn, PO Box 1, Kirkcaldy, Fife KY1 2SB; tel: 01592 643111 – manufacturers of linoleum and cushioned vinyl flooring

Forbo Lancaster, Lune Mills, Lancaster LA1 5QN; tel: 01524 65222 – manufacturers of children's wallcoverings and fabrics

Foundation for the Study of Infant Deaths, 14 Halkin Street, London SW1X 7DP; tel: 0171–235 0965 – information on reducing the risk of cot death; baby's room thermometer available price £2.50, send cheque made out to FSID Sales

Harris/Mulhouse, LG Harris & Co., Stoke Prior, Bromsgrove, Worcestershire B60 4AE; tel: 01527 575441

Harrison Drape, Bradford Street, Birmingham B12 0PE; tel: 0121–766 6111 – manufacturers of curtain tracks and poles

Hulsta, 22 Bruton Street, London W1X 7DA; tel: 0171–629 4881 – manufacturers and suppliers of children's fitted bedroom furniture

IKEA Department Store, 255 North Circular Road, London NW10 0JQ; tel: 0181–451 5566 – suppliers of children's furniture

International Paint, 24–30 Canute Road, Southampton, Hampshire SO14 3PB; tel: 01703 226722 – manufacturers of child-safe lacquer and matt-black blackboard paint

John Lewis, 278–306 Oxford Street, London W1A 1EX; tel: 0171–629 7711 – lighting, sheeting and other fabrics by the metre, decorating materials, general furnishings and non-slip rug underlay; call for addresses of other branches

Laura Ashley, 150 Bath Road, Maidenhead, Berks SL6 4YS; tel: 01628 770345 – suppliers of children's fabrics and wallpapers; call for addresses of nearest branches

Luxaflex, Hunter Douglas, The Industrial Estate, Larkhall, Lanarkshire ML9 2PD; tel: 01698 881281 – suppliers of made-to-measure and ready-made blinds of all types

Mamas & Papas, Colne Bridge Road, Huddersfield, West Yorks HD5 0RH; tel: 01484 438222 – manufacturers of cots, mattresses, highchairs, playpens, prams and pushchairs

Mothercare, Head Office, Cherry Tree Road, Watford, Herts WD2 5SH; tel: 01923 210210 (call for your nearest branch) – suppliers of all types of nursery equipment and furnishings, useful catalogue

The National Bed Federation, 251 Brompton Road, London SW3 2EZ; tel: 0171–589 4888 – advice on the purchase of beds, including bunk beds

The Nursery Window, 83 Walton Street, London SW3 2HP; tel: 0171–581 3358 – fabrics and wallpapers for children, plus some accessories

The Quilt Room, 20 West Street, Dorking, Surrey RH14 1BL; tel: 01306 740739 – fantastic selection of quilt fabrics, wadding and sewing equipment; mail order service

Readicut Wool Co. Ltd., PO Box 1, Terry Mills, Ossett, W. Yorks WF5 9SA; tel: 01924 810810 – mail order suppliers of rug-making materials and kits

Relyon, Wellington, Somerset TA21 8NN; tel: 01823 667501 – manufacturers of beds, including stacking beds

Rufflette, Sharston Road, Wythenshawe, Manchester M22 4TH; tel: 0161–998 1811 – manufacturers of curtain heading tapes and hooks

Sharps Bedrooms, Albany Park, Frimley, Camberley, Surrey GU15 2PL; tel: 01276 802000 – fitted children's bedroom furniture

Spur Shelving, Spur House, Otterspool Way, Watford, Herts WD2 8HT; tel: 01923 226071 – manufacturers of adjustable shelving brackets

The Stencil Store, 20–21 Heronsgate Road, Chorley Wood, Rickmansworth, Herts WD3 5BN; tel: 01923 285577 – suppliers of stencils, stencilling equipment, brushes for paint effects and pre-tinted decorative glazes by mail order

Vymura, PO Box 15, Talbot Road, Hyde, Cheshire SK14 4EJ; tel: 0161–368 4000 – manufacturers of children's wallcoverings and fabrics

INDEX

Page numbers in italic refer to illustrations

PICTURE CREDITS

The publishers would like to thank the following for
their kind help in supplying photographs:

Frontispiece: Mothercare

Chapter 1
Page 6: Designers Guild
Page 7: Laura Ashley
Page 11: Dulux Paints
Page 15 (left): Dulux Paints
Page 15 (right): Boras

Chapter 2
Page 18 (left): Elizabeth Whiting Associates
Pages 18/19: Akzo Nobel Decorative Coatings
Page 23: Dulux Paints
Page 26: Harris/Mulhouse
Page 31: Elizabeth Whiting Associates
Page 35: Vymura
Page 38: Vymura
Page 43: Forbo-Lancaster

Chapter 3
Page 46: Forbo Nairn
Page 47: The Nursery Window
Page 50 (top and bottom): Elizabeth Whiting
   Associates

Chapter 4
Page 55: Harrison Drape
Page 58: Designers Guild
Page 62: The Stencil Store
Page 63: Luxaflex

Chapter 5
Page 67: Elizabeth Whiting Associates
Page 70: Cover Charm

Chapter 6
Page 74 (left): The Nursery Window
Pages 74/5: Sharps Bedrooms
Page 78: Harris/Mulhouse
Page 79: Spur Shelving
Page 82: Hulsta
Page 83: Boots
Page 86: IKEA
Page 87: Stencil Artists
Page 90: Crown Wallcoverings
Page 91 (top): Crown Paints
Page 91 (bottom): Fairfax

Chapter 7
Page 99: Mothercare

Chapter 8
Pages 106/107: Dulux Paints
Page 111: Designers Guild
Page 119: Laura Ashley
Page 122: Elizabeth Whiting Associates

Many people helped me directly and indirectly with this book. I would like to thank Mike Vickers for his very valuable assistance in compiling the painting and wallpapering sections, (thanks, Mike!) and thanks too to Susan Duff, Jane Page, Jean Shapiro and Jerry Tubby for their helpful advice. I would also like to thank Jessica Alexander at The National Bed Federation for her help with the section on bunk beds. And thanks, too, to everyone who so patiently put up with me during the months while I was writing this book! I would also like to thank everyone who lent me transparencies and who supplied me with information.